Inspirational Guidance Towards a New Era

*Channelled Messages from the
Archangel Metatron*

PLANET EARTH
A New Way of Being - A New Way of Healing

Inspirational Guidance Towards a New Era

Channelled Messages from the Archangel Metatron

Metatron's Cube

Channelled by Ann-Marie Campbell-Smith

First paperback edition 2023

Cover Design by Juan Padron

Sacred geometry symbols – Metatron's Cube, Flower of Life: iStock.com/Natasha_Chuen – back cover, inside pages

978-1-80541-360-8 (paperback)

978-1-80541-361-5 (ebook)

www.sourcelightconnection.co.uk

Disclaimer

This book does not contain medical advice. The information provided in this book is for general information only and is not a substitute for professional medical or health advice. Always seek guidance from a medical / health professional. The use of or reliance upon any information contained in this book is solely at the reader's risk and under no circumstances will the author, channel or publisher of this book have any liability to the reader for any loss, claim or damage of any kind incurred as a result of the use or misuse of this book or reliance on any information, statement or suggestions provided within it.

Dedicated to all across the ages
who have found themselves on
planet Earth and asked,

'Who am I? Why am I here?'

ACKNOWLEDGMENTS

Huge gratitude and thanks to my dear friends, Anya Rose, who alerted me to the opportunity to receive Archangel Metatron's words and gave continued encouragement and help, and Mary Irene, who helped to share the writings early on and offered valuable feedback.

My grateful thanks to Paul and to Rhea, my beloved husband and daughter; fellow travellers and companions across millennia and recurrent sources of challenge, learning and joy. Your enduring support, encouragement, love, good sense and wisdom perpetually sustain me.
I honour and love you both.

CONTENTS

Archangel Metatron did not give a title for all messages prior to relaying the detail. Therefore this list gives titles (with initial capitals) as supplied by Metatron or otherwise the opening phrase of the message. Please note that these headings are not necessarily a precise indication of the message content but are offered for referencing and identification purposes.

PREFACE

Channelled Messages from the Archangel Metatron

This document is a collection of channelled messages gifted to us from the Archangel Metatron, said to be the 'king of the angels', the scribe who takes down God's words, and the one who deals with transition and evolution across the universes.

Archangel Metatron has asked that information be made available setting out, in straightforward terms, what is happening now on planet Earth, why it is happening, our role in these events as they unfold, and how we can all help to bring in the required changes quickly, evolving ourselves into the bright, enlightened and masterful cosmic beings that is our true nature in the process.

Of this aspect of his role Archangel Metatron states:
(1 September 2021)

I am Metatron. I am the great architect of the shift on planet Earth from the third dimension to the fifth dimension – and beyond, as most beings on Earth at this time come from the higher dimensions. I am orchestrating the changes on planet Earth with the help of other, very many, beings of light and love from across the universe, from the other universes, to help and assist on planet Earth at this time. It is a major undertaking. All on planet Earth are blessed indeed to be participants, although only a few of you fully understand the significance of the work, the effort, you are putting in to achieve this shift, and its importance.

Read these messages and see what resonates with you, uplifts you. It will help to ignite a light within you, and to shift your light to a higher level and help to move you onwards and upwards towards understanding and taking on your role on planet Earth at this time.

I was privileged to receive more than eighty channelled messages from the Archangel Metatron, relayed to me over a period January to October 2021. Information, the words, given to me whilst connected with Archangel Metatron is printed in italics. Where I have felt it appropriate I have requested clarification or confirmation of 'truth' from Archangel Metatron. Where statement offered in the channellings does not resonate with you then please follow your own guidance regarding what you believe to be the case, **your truth**.

There are instances in these messages where a 'you' as the subject becomes a 'we'. Metatron states: *You are still channelling my energy. Sometimes the 'we' does include myself, Metatron, and the light being collective for we have all taken on responsibility to planet Earth and mankind's ascension, so some of what is discussed, being relayed, does apply to us all in this project.*

Ann-Marie Campbell-Smith

November 2022

INTRODUCTION

Blessed and Mighty Archangel Metatron (30 January 2021)

This is the beginning of a new phase in the annals of planet Earth. There is much to discuss. Much will change now and soon. We need to change the way that Earth manifests the will of God, the will of the Divine. You are all here for beautiful purpose. A divine purpose. You need to pull together to achieve this now. Many of you have sharp recollection of why you are here and what you have come here to do. Others have no awareness still – caught up in the dramas of the third dimensional collective running on borrowed time. There are patterns to this progression towards the light, seen in other places where the light comes through to right and rectify the progression towards the Divine.

We are at a crossroads. We can heal this planet, together. We can build a new future for this magnificent jewel of the cosmos. Such beauty here, a beauty most on this planet do not appreciate fully in that it is one of the most amazingly rich and wonderful terrains in this universe. You are all so blessed. Wars and acrimony from many thousands of years past, affecting much of this universe, have destroyed original purpose in this experiment on planet Earth, which related to light and love and the exercise of free will in circumstances where it is not usually allowed to have free rein; choice in all things. We created a cataclysm. Now it is the time of reparation after much work by and in the name of the divine one who is the creator of all things and whose will is paramount and will not be undone / opposed.

The great lord Lucifer attempted to subvert the Will of God and divide his fine creation, deposing mankind into the pits of darkness without access to the glory of the redeeming lights of creation and the mighty creator of all. [Lucifer, 'prince of darkness', became so because he wanted to stop light getting through to mankind who he believed 'didn't deserve it as they were not 'high' beings'.] *For this he has been cast away, cast asunder, as his was not God's plan. Now, we extricate the fine beauty of planet Earth from the hands of the evil ones who have no love for God, although they protest that this is not so. Many here are confused and follow the evil ones in their darkness, bewitched by logic and resolute 'good sense' which sees them follow as lemmings over an edge into the abyss below. They are blinded in the darkness and do not see or understand the light that is God, and goodness. They are deceived by 'fine things' and 'noble aspirations' which are worthless in the great scheme for planet Earth and serve only to perpetuate the great lie that is embodied in this world and its civilisation.*

All this is about to change. The lie to be exposed and true order, the purpose and the plan, to be restored. Joy to return to all who tread this beautiful Earth.

We all now have a job to do. Tasks to undertake, no matter whether we reside on planet Earth or are one of the 144,000 beings of light who are assisting mankind through this process, this progress, towards the light and to achieving God's Will on Earth. Many in the universe have taken on responsibility to restore correct order in the plan for Earth and others come to help at certain times and junctures, for example when cosmic alignments favour certain steps or actions to be taken. It is all indeed a Great Master Plan. We are all privileged and joyful to be working as part of it and indeed now that it is coming to fulfilment there is much celebration and jubilation in this universe and beyond.

We need to heal this planet of its desecration that has been allowed to occur. We need to heal the beings residing on this planet so that they can move into their true roles at this time. Many will have come here to help and to heal planet Earth, whose soul is Gaia.

We are all invested in the restoration of planet Earth to her original purpose and pristine beauty and purity. Many animal species who came to populate this amazing land, with agreement on order of hierarchy, have now completed their roles and purpose here and will go, becoming extinct as part of the natural order.

As mankind hones its abilities to connect telepathically with the animal and plant kingdoms we will discover and re-discover ways and approaches to resolving many of the challenges we face in terms of planetary pollution and environmental damage. Animals, plants and elementals will effectively share with us in non-verbal communication ways in which we can assist them to thrive once again. They will 'tell' us exactly what we need to do in order to help. Elemental beings will play a major part too as they also are enjoying the onset of a changing world which for some is an awakening in much the same way as mankind is waking up to truth and reality.

Some people are now realising that they can 'speak' the language of the dolphins and this basis for understanding will open up the realm of the seas to helpful communication to cleanse and purify.

The restoration of planet Earth will indeed be a joint effort of unity of purpose and love.

We all have different talents, skills and abilities to enable us to carry out all the tasks that we came here to undertake. Some are very specialised and some demand a more general array of knowledge and awareness. We are often led to other things as our work and understanding progresses. Do not envy or be jealous of someone else's apparent abundance of role. We are all equally important at this time.

The way of life on this planet will be very different before the decade is up. No longer the pain, the infighting, the conflicts and the bloodshed which has characterised every society at some point over aeons; unrelenting destruction and desecration.

So, What is the Purpose of this Document?

*These channelled writings aim to set hope in the hearts of the many who are afraid and don't understand what is happening on planet Earth at this time. Many who understand and see that there is change, and welcome it, neither see, appreciate nor are aware of the massive import on a galactic scale of the immense changes and times that planet Earth and her voyagers are living through. For Earth is a living being, Gaia (*and is herself evolving*).*

These writings *intend to explain what people need to do and can do on a personal level to find equilibrium, healing and joy in this passage of Earth's journey.*

It will explain who they are, where they came from and what they are doing on this planet – or certainly a general picture of what they came to do; the principles of their existence and purpose here.

It will set out steps that they can take; things to look at within themselves that will lead them into the light and a new, happier, more constructive and positive way of being. It will help them to unlock the truth of who they are, what they are and what they came to planet Earth to undertake and achieve. For all have purpose, a mighty, divine purpose on planet Earth – Mother Earth – at this beautiful wondrous time in her cycle of days.

We are in wondrous, magnificent times of love, splendour, joy and marvellous achievement. A true cosmic plan is in play on planet Earth at this time. This document needs to, and will, convey this. It will inspire people and set out some important markers to help them transition into the light. Their awareness and growing knowledge and understanding of the nature of light will lead them forward in many ways in their lives – practical, emotional, spiritual and in their purpose. It is all about the light.

It will set out guidance for how they can interact with their families, their colleagues and the community around them. How best to counter the problems that people are finding themselves in, in these days of new beginnings. It will aim to offer prompts in all respects.

It will show and explain how right thinking can help the many forms of life around them. Indicate what they can do to make a difference. Help them to understand why the planet is under pressure; how animals and the Earth respond to the pressures exerted on them by humankind's actions, and essentially 'how it all works; why it is going 'wrong' and what can be done by every one of you as individuals'.

It will inspire, energise, revitalise and motivate. Help to restore health and a positive outlook; to identify original purpose and the job 'we' signed up for. The wonder of being on planet Earth at this remarkable time.

Suggestions on How to use this Document

Archangel Metatron indicates that these passages are potential routes into higher consciousness, expanded awareness, and a pathway forward for our selves. They hold keys and codes to unlock and instigate thoughts and actions, often subliminally, but all for our highest good. Much is waiting to be unlocked and accessed, when the time is right.

Before you open the book you may wish to ask that it will reflect to you what you need at that particular time, and that it paves the way towards your perfect future. You might open a page at random, or scan the contents list and see what you feel drawn to. The messages are generally presented in the order in which they were received. If you feel guided to read them in this order then follow that guidance.

Before you read your chosen passage ask to absorb its aspects that are important for you at that time and to be shown any 'hidden' information. You will be gifted so much more beyond the words and the essence. Remember that all is love, all is perfect, even though it may not seem so according to our perceptions at the time.

You might wish to meditate upon, go deeper into, what you have read - or follow up a reference, phrase, idea, or word you feel drawn towards.

Above all, follow your intuition. It knows what is 'right' for you.

Archangel Metatron has said that all reading this book are under his care and tutelage and will be taken care of and protected.

Grace and Forgiveness

Grace is a gift of God. Grace is bestowed upon those who show themselves worthy of dispensation of light from the Divine and higher beings of light and awareness. We can ask for blessings on our fellows, which is a form of grace.

Grace comes to the heart, opens it and fills it with glory and a sense of joy and contentment, an awareness that all is well and will be well. A sense of forgiveness, understanding and knowledge that we are understood - that our fears and worries, hopes and expectations, are known and understood. Sympathy extended for our losses and any sadness at any parts of our lives that may not be working well or as we might have wished them to flow. A form of forgiveness, and deliverance from any guilt or sense of shortcoming in our strivings to do well in our lives on this planet and to 'be good', living in accordance with the standards we expect of ourselves and believe God, or any higher authority, would wish us to adhere to / comply with.

A state of grace is one of equanimity in which peace is sustained; acceptance of what 'is', however that 'is' has come to be. Knowledge that one is accepted and if necessary forgiven for any misdeeds or shortcoming in the sight of God. Grace is something that we might need to consider offering - as forgiveness - to others who may have complicated our lives in some way.

Forgiveness releases not just the person we forgive but ourselves too. Releases us into joy, love and gives us freedom from our past. We are set free to look once again, and more fully, into the future and to grasp with both hands and embrace the wonderful things that life and the world around us may wish to offer to us.

Forgiveness heals wounds of the soul. It allows us to close a door on events, reduces our karmic debt and liberates us. We are free to allow more light into our being, to see the world in a new light. Anger, hatred, resentment are like blights upon our soul and upon our lives; dark entities that will turn on us and devour us if we allow them life by dwelling upon them and thereby feeding them, and sustaining them. Focus therefore only on those things that you wish to grow and increase in your life, not on those things that you do not want.

Hawaiian Ho'oponopono Huna Prayer for healing - use to assist / enable forgiveness

When you are in conflict with someone you may see only what is evident in this life, on the surface. There is possibly a deeper reason why you may seem to be in conflict with another human being, and this could be related to a shared past life, or a 'soul contract' where roles are played out in this lifetime as a means to provide learning experience or to resolve karmic debt. The Hawaiian Huna prayer – Ho'oponopono - has the power to resolve deeper issues we may not be aware of. It is not always necessary to understand / find the root causes of the 'scenario'. Consciously repeat the prayer whilst focusing on the 'situation' with the aim that it be resolved for the highest good of all parties and that all may move forward. 'I am sorry, please forgive me, I love you, thank you.'

The time has come for all on planet Earth to change. *All beings, all life forms. We are all part of God. The birds, bees, plant life, animals, sea creatures, elementals, man – Adam Kadmon as he is known in the universe. The Great Experiment that almost failed. We are with you all. Your time has come to shine and to bring forth into the light, under the light, the glory that is yours, for you have all helped to bring about the amazing changes that are now unfolding in this world. Over lifetimes you have worked to hone yourselves into creatures that can now, at this pivotal point in the aeons of time, embrace the light of the Divine and all it offers you to metamorphose into crystalline beings that **are** light; refract and reflect that light, for light is **all that is**. Blessed, you are the light. We are all the light. Now, you must come to know this and to be this.*

Put down your swords, your knives and guns and embrace all those around you. Weapons and hatred achieve only to increase the conflict. Forgiveness, love, and acceptance that we are all part of God are the only tools that achieve lasting peace. These are the new 'weapons' of choice for the enlightened, those beings that truly understand their position in this galaxy and that we must stop running around in circles, cycles of despair, and bring in a new way of being on Earth. One which respects and recognises all life as sacred.

This beautiful planet too is moving forward. Just as humankind has met its final crisis, this Earth, Gaia, is also in crisis. She too is now moving into the great light, as she shifts her position within the stars, and all on planet Earth now, and those who will be coming shortly to this planet, are avowed to help her to do this. She cannot fulfil this change, ascend to her new positioning and placement in the galaxy, without our help. We too, on Earth, must ascend into this new placement, this new way of being, with her. We must therefore ascend too. We are all one. We are one with all other beings; we are one with our planet.

Trust. You may ask yourself, 'What is this? Is this a new religion? Is this wishful thinking?' It is neither. It is the word of God. The Divine Plan for planet Earth. You are part of that plan. A part of you knows and understands this, for you have come here, incarnated here consciously, in order to carry out your role in that plan. You may ask, 'How do I find out what I am supposed to be doing here?' You may well have asked yourself that already, as you travel through life, unaware that you have your own special mission here. That we all have a special mission here...

You may look at yourself as a being who has faults, imperfections, may not have always acted nobly, kindly, or even as 'good', and ask, 'Why would I be part of any divine mission on Earth?' Know that we all have faults, failings, have done unpleasant things in past lives and maybe in this life.

[We have seen] War, division, conflict, conflagration; pitted against each other by forces of darkness that promote, feed and revel in division and create disharmony, distrust, destruction - and ultimately disintegration of life on this planet.

Be as One. You are all beings of light. Now is the time for you to progress, upgrade if you like. To metamorphose into a being of immense light and at the same time save the planet and enable her to metamorphose also. Together we can do this. Unity is the key and the way forward for us all. Unity of self, community and of planet Earth. It is time to be unified and united in common purpose.

We are all unique beings.

The Beauty of Being

All beings on planet Earth breathe in order to feed their bodies with the pristine substance that keeps them alive – oxygen; sometimes CO_2. Breathing is not a function that every sentient being in the universe has experienced. Possessing a body is not something every sentient being has experienced. Bodies offer (incarnate) immense learning tools for all their occupants! Limitations, specially honed abilities (physical and mental) that allow them to excel in different ways and explore, as specialists, certain aspects of life, their surroundings, and the nature of being. Also warnings when their way of thinking or the way in which they use their body is not honouring and looking after that body and / or the divine being inside it.

Mankind has choice and the physical body / incarnation provides a means to show its occupant what works / doesn't work and to attempt to ensure they maintain an appropriate way of life to retain health of mind and body, ie optimise their approach to life and thought.

We are all beings of immense light, love and purity. That is our core, the divine essence that the mighty creator has imbued us with. You beings on planet Earth are no exception to this. Many of you are now awakening to this awareness. (You just haven't all awoken to this awareness yet, although of course this is now changing, and changing very quickly indeed.) You are all fine, beautiful beings of light whose purpose is to transform planet Earth from its current perilous state to that of beauty, peace and safety for all sentient beings. A restoration process. Don't doubt your abilities. Many of you incarnated with the purpose to be light workers – to help to bring in the essence of this awareness of the incoming New Golden Age.

You will all need to work collectively, in harmony, to do this work. You will succeed. You have all elected to be on this planet at this time to undertake these vitally important roles. One problem with planet Earth, however, is that as you incarnate to take up your body you forget all the details of why you have come here, what you are doing and are to do; your role. The information about the role you are coming to fulfil is blanked from your mind, and so as you grow up and develop you may have a 'feeling', a slight awareness that you are here for some purpose, some 'mission'; something in the back of your mind... but no real clue as to what it is. It makes things somewhat difficult! It is part of the process, the package if you like, that offers mankind free will on planet Earth. So you are here, and you have a job to do (ie a divine purpose job rather than the 'day-job', although they may coincide, and happily this is now the likelihood with the incoming, new way of being). You just don't know what that divine job is or what it involves.

Mankind has been incarnating on planet Earth for aeons. With a few exceptions most of us have been in training for this current *incarnation where we put all the work, all our learning, into practice over a relatively short space in time to arise and emerge from the 'old' ways of being, where we [may] have tended to exploit everything and every being around us, into a new era of love, light, respect for the planet and for all sentient beings that she hosts. Of course this change is already happening.*

Millions of people on this planet are already aware of their specific purpose in these momentous times and have been preparing the way, laying foundations, for these massive changes on Earth. Young people are coming in with a much closer, quicker, connection to the planet and to their roles and are adding momentum to these changes. They see the world through very different eyes, as they join in as this great movement is in progress, and instinctively recognise what needs to be done, incarnating with the benefit of a new perspective on the planet and its muddled, muddied governance. These troops have for the most part done all their training and are ready to go!

Using Light to Heal

Light is the source of healing. From time to time the quality of light available to and reflected / channelled to planet Earth is upgraded, bathing all beings in beautiful luminescence which some can see, some consciously utilise, and many, most, are oblivious to. It matters not in this last respect as all living beings benefit from the light of the cosmos. Their very cells sense the light quality and respond, sensing actually that the essence of the creator is intensifying, opening up these very cells to greater opportunities and possibilities.

All aspects of our body – physical, mental, emotional, spiritual (consciousness) - respond. These specific, particular responses in individuals vary enormously depending upon their stage of development, awakening to and awareness of the wider cosmic picture of life. In some cases the great light heightens existing spirituality and unlocks doors to even more sublime levels of being and co-operation. In others the awakening sensitivity to a greater sense of 'being' causes some confusion and promotes unease. This is in individuals who scarcely understand or believe that they are beings of consciousness, let alone that they are mighty, and aspects of the divine creator; that they have a role here on Earth and in the cosmos that they consciously volunteered to do and take up, in this lifetime, on planet Earth.

So the light uplifts, and also unsettles. Our very inner beings react and respond to it. Light is the source, the underlying truth, of everything in this universe.

This document is about using light to heal. Also, because everything is light, it is about natural healing in its many aspects.

Light is a component of everything. Light heals the light in other things; 'like heals like'. It restores the light it encounters to a higher, purer light. Where light finds light it can restore it to the brighter light of the purity and intensity of the new light.

Colour represents the differing vibrations of light. Light also balances. When we send light we are balancing and restoring harmony and right working / correct functioning of individual aspects of the various systems which interplay in life forms. Light... soft light... induces different moods. Colour is a reflection of different vibrations of light. Laser cuts and eliminates. We are light and light work is in harmony with all life.

Light is a life form. It has consciousness. We can speak to the light, directly.

Beings of increasing purity of light; we can draw them close to us and they will help us. We can invoke them to participate in the healings. They will merge with us.

Diet, water, impurities. Light can change molecules – we can heal everything. Light purifies us by upgrading / lessening our density; the cells respond and harmonise; the unease / dis-ease is cleared.

In certain places - like Lourdes for example - conditions exist which allow a higher purity of light to flow into the area and to be utilised. Light cleanses light so all is purified in that area to a clearer, higher level.

We stand in front of beings and reflect the light into them. Purer beings come into us and act as mirrors; or we are mirroring the light into them. These beings will merge into us and import increasing levels of purity into us.

*Once we have foreign bodies in the natural physical body we cannot restore in the same way. We must neutralise their effects and **then** restore / introduce the light. Neutralisation of not just the pain / side effects but of the 'machinery' as well.*

Light affects the integrity of matter.

The spiritual light quotient – of everything – is very important.

*It **is** all about the light.*

The Ages of Man

Mankind's development on planet Earth has been characterised by different beings of different levels of capability and aptitude, suited to the cycle of planet Earth and the lessons to be learned at any stage. At times this development cycle has been taken advantage of by beings from outside [extra-terrestrial] who are not of pure light or love. This has caused problems at various stages, and the planetary brotherhoods have needed to step in at various stages to correct the pathway. Much has gone on behind the scenes, so to speak, to bring mankind to its current position. Many of you have been called in from other planetary systems throughout the cosmos, as volunteers, to assist on planet Earth and help at this time.

Mankind is now in the process of a fundamental change in physicality from the flesh and blood that you know to a structure crystalline in nature. A truly magnificent evolution. Nowhere in the cosmos does this structure yet exist in quite the same form. This structure absorbs light and reflects light and is sentient. (You know that the solidity of objects is a perspective that is held on planet Earth and other third dimensional density planets, and that this is illusion. Nothing is solid.)

Mankind, along with planet Earth, is moving into the fifth dimension, and the body that holds this consciousness will need to change, indeed **is** *changing; The DNA has 12 strands rather than three and as this aspect of body changes we will change along with it. Our need for water will increase, our tastes for food will change, naturally seeking out wholesome sustenance that nourishes rather than merely satisfies. But the food, the plants, will be changing also along with the planet – and everything on and around it – so there will be different food 'options', if you like, as new species of plant (or those* *familiar to the times of Atlantis) will re-establish themselves. A bit like 'manna'; wholesome, delicious, 'complete' food 'of the Gods', gifted to humankind. Water is vital and will become more so. Many of you say you 'don't like' water. Partly this is because of the cleansing processes necessary due to planetary conditions. As the planet purifies, and the water she offers along with it, the taste of water will be restored and it will be delightful to drink. It will be a 'liquor of the Gods'.*

The higher vibration of the fifth dimensional body will require purer food and water and a lighter diet. The heavy dense foods that humankind has been eating in the third dimension, such as meat, will not suit the fifth dimensional body in any way. Meat will be perceived as unsuitable or even unclean due to its nature and origins. Meat may be eaten with the permission of the animal concerned (as North American Indians requested permission of the buffalo to hunt them for food) *but eating our animal brethren will become less and less common.*

Our fifth dimensional crystalline bodies will change both in structure and nature. Apart from the DNA change there will be fewer bones, fewer teeth, reduced musculature. Our eyes may enlarge and will shine brighter. Different coloured irises will enable different aspects of light to be detected and absorbed. Our nervous systems will be refined and we will be able to regrow digits and even limbs over time.

Our fifth dimensional bodies will not show dis-ease [disease] as they do now (dis-ease of human psyche will dramatically reduce as the planetary and society changes flourish) and our bodies will once again be able to heal themselves of any imbalances. We will have the awareness and capacity to monitor our own bodies and correct any potential issues long before disease manifests, and when problems do arise they will be generally corrected by healers without fuss or major intervention. All will be joy!

Quite naturally, our fifth dimensional bodies will reflect and assist the new way of being that the planetary shift will bring to us. Our perceptions will be finer and more acute (the 'sixth sense' becoming far more evident) and we will become aware of much around us that has previously been obscured. Notably, the elemental beings of the plant and nature kingdom, and our abilities to communicate with elementals, plants and animals and with sea creatures – most importantly the whales, dolphins and sharks who perform important roles in balancing the oceanic biosphere. The disruption of the marine environment through certain scientific endeavours is pushing Mother Earth to dangerous limits of what she can endure, as the assistance of the whales and dolphins is limited and damaged by electropollution; plus these beings are being hunted to extinction. In our ignorance and ego we are destroying our planet, our beautiful home.

We will sense more acutely the feelings and thoughts of those around us, and we will increasingly find ourselves communicating telepathically with fellow humans as well as with all other life forms. Thought travels faster than light so we will easily communicate across the world and, indeed, across the cosmos as we rediscover our own individual heritages and our origins.

As our awareness and understanding grows we will be gifted knowledge by benign beings of light who currently surround us invisibly (they are on different dimensions). This will initially help us to cleanse and purify our planet, and then later on will assist and enable the adoption here of the new ways of being. Our lives will transform hugely, but the change will come naturally as we undergo massive and collective evolution.

The Crystal Beings of Light

Our thoughts, our perspective, give things around us form. Form is sometimes solid, dense, sometimes liquid and sometimes the softest impression of a different light quality in the air; a shaft, a wisp, a light shadow. As we gain entry into higher dimensions of being our perspective refines, heightens indeed, and we 'see'/ become aware of new qualities of light and visibility. After all, everything is light.

In truth, our capacity to see and envision is boundless, limited only by our own imagination and our individual concepts of 'what is' and what 'can be' or 'might be'.

There are many demons around this world, this Earth. *But they are being quieted now. In their final throes… The many words and actions of love and light by the chosen brethren are bringing this world, this planet, into golden light of awareness, hope, peace and sanctity.*

Look around. You may not believe it but the truth is drawing into people's hearts. They instinctively recognise what is right and many now have the courage to embrace love, to choose love over the mutterings of those who would perpetuate the havoc and the hatred for mischievous ends. The demons are fleeing. Their time is over. Blessings and love to all who promote and work with the light, who represent our mighty creator God on planet Earth and in the mighty wondrous realms of the cosmos and the multiverse.

So what now?

*We need to heal and cleanse the mighty divisions in the races of man on this planet so that all might live in harmony, love and contentment, abiding by the laws of God, the Law of One, as God intended. The fragmentation of opinion has created much strife and suffering on this planet. Indeed, those who ardently follow 'their' truth and speak it to others, asking them to conform to **their** view, have perpetuated, even instigated, much of the disharmony and destruction. History confirms this.*

So, again, what now?

The demons that prowl and pollute our beautiful planet Earth are returning to whence they came. As the light energy and purity of this planet rises they can no longer remain; they scuttle back to the darkness. They will be purified in time. They now yet have a day on Earth.

So, what now?

Love. Love, caring, understanding, tolerance, forbearance. Beauty, wonder, marvels, virtue, clarity, goodness, responsibility. Responsibility for ourselves and for others; to ourselves and to others, to bring in and accept the light into our bodies, our minds, to raise our purity, to raise our awareness, to clear out the trash from our minds, our lives, our planet and to bring in and embrace purity, clarity, love, light, understanding and acceptance. Acceptance that we are all part of the creator of all things; God, Source, and that we are here on planet Earth with a job to do. The most important job in the history of this planet.

Healing the Divides; Healing Ourselves

We need to heal ourselves before we can heal the divisions between us.

Healing comes to us in many ways. There are many different channels to healing; many different routes. We heal in different ways according to our individual psyches, our understanding and how we see the world around us. Also [in] our soul's journey over what might be many, many lifetimes, some here on planet Earth and some elsewhere in other star systems, in different types of consciousness.

Our individual journeys to this point are unique; our individual situations highly complex. We are all, however, part of the one-ness, the unity of Source. This unity of Source pervades the universe. Don't be mistaken, there are conflicts and divisions in other areas of this grand cosmos where the peoples of planetary systems have warred against each other and the inhabitants of other star systems; places where there are divisions, places where there are memories of past hurt.

Conscious life forms in the surrounding solar system in our galaxy, and light consciousness anchored on neighbouring planets - Jupiter, Venus, Uranus and Neptune - are keen to help us to now overcome all the difficulties we face, to heal our divisions, unite the factions; unite consciousness on this planet – people, animal and sea life, plant life, elementals, Gaia herself. For we all come from the one Source. Our cosmic brethren are here to help us to do this, to guide us. And if we don't all act together and pull together they will, in love, step in and 'force' us to do this. That would save planet Earth but it would be a great sadness for all of us, who have all volunteered to come here at this time, that we have failed to act appropriately, failed to unite and save the Blue Jewel of this galaxy and of the universe.

The Value of Change

Many people dislike change. Some people thrive on it – the excitement of the new and unexplained, the opportunities for new experiences, new connections, new places, new lessons, new understanding; a new life maybe, and new purpose, a new outlook.

That is what the current planetary changes are offering to all on planet Earth at this time. The opportunity to do almost everything very differently. To discard the sorrow and strife and move into a new way of being characterised by love for oneself, and all around us, and a unity of purpose to create a world and societies based on mutual respect, love for all beings, a common purpose for the highest good of all. Societies where all people have value and are able to contribute according to their skills and talents and where all are taken care of in their time of need. A society of kindness and care for all beings; 'Heaven on Earth' – no, really, Heaven on Earth will be our creation. Heaven as we understand it (the fifth dimensional Garden of Eden) will be enabled to flourish here on planet Earth.

How is this Going to Happen?

The change to a new society of love and unity is already happening, already well under way. Currently what is no longer required is being dismantled, much of it forcibly. It's a bit like a spring clean of planet Earth – except it hasn't been done for millennia and we have allowed an awful lot of rubbish to accumulate – both in the minds and attitudes of mankind and in the way we have trashed and continue to trash the still-beautiful planet and destroy many of the life forms it has supported. This cannot continue.

Unseen forces of love, light and wisdom are manoeuvring the actions and events that are bringing about these massive changes on planet

Earth. Natural events – natural disasters as you may refer to them – are wrought by planet Earth herself as she attempts to continue to balance the stresses and strains mankind's actions have placed on her. Gaia is a living being and needs certain conditions in the atmosphere, seas and on land masses to continue to support life forms on this planet and allow them to co-exist in harmony and in equilibrium. We need to address everything that is undermining planetary equilibrium right now.

The [Covid-19] pandemic has stopped what was the current way of life on planet Earth in its tracks. Covid has forced a halt on so many aspects of 21st century life that were destructive to the planet and given everyone, worldwide, the opportunity to stop and take stock. It offers people time and space to look at events and respond to them with the benefits of an open heart. 'Insisting' now that we are all not 'too busy' to ensure that these issues are dealt with properly.

We are moving to a cleaner planet and kinder, more united, societies all over the world – although some areas will be able to adapt and change quicker than others.

The Great Invocation – Alice Bailey, 1937

'*May light and love and power restore the Plan on Earth*' [extract / final line of invocation].

Now is the time for the restoration of the 'Plan on Earth'. Now is the time when mankind arises from the depths and density of the darkness, confusion and denseness it has been dwelling in for the past ten thousand years and ascends into the light, purity, love and unity of the fifth dimension, a place or 'state of being' which operates very differently to the third dimension in which it has previously existed. All is well.

How is this Happening?

The societal structures which no longer serve this greater being - which is a sovereign being that is its own master and does not require leaders or people in charge to dictate how it lives - are falling apart. These societal structures have been based on fear rather than love to a greater or lesser extent; depends upon where you live. Now that the hearts of all beings on planet Earth are open, love is to rule. We will run our societies based on love, unity, co-operation and equity. No-one needs to be in charge because all is heart-based, all have open hearts receiving and sending out love at all times. The ego is relinquished, gone – or very nearly so. All are in harmony and united in purpose. Greed, envy, pride fall way – they have no foundation. Many live by the Law of One.

Very soon you will begin to notice, if you haven't already, that people who embrace and live in this light of love and one-ness are displaying skills thought either impossible or demonstrated only by psychics or those who have dedicated lifetimes to learning these skills – teleportation, telepathy, levitation, 'remote viewing' and so on.

Actually we are all capable of these skills. We have been practicing them for aeons in other places, other planets, as other entities in this amazing cosmos.

The thing about planet Earth – the sorrow of planet Earth – is that we forget that we have these abilities when we come here, and the density of the third dimension doesn't make it easy for most of us to demonstrate or to realise that we have these latent skills. Sometimes they come through in random moments, and we wonder at the 'specialness' of these occasions. The truth is that we can all do these things but that we don't believe or understand this, and that tends to block our abilities to replicate and demonstrate with ease.

*The plan is to make planet Earth fifth dimensional – **now** – and all her occupants the same. A wonderful new future, a new way of being for us all.*

Attempts to return to 'normal' will only frustrate people and perpetuate the pandemics, the plagues, the extinctions, the eruptions, the floods, the fires, as planet Earth struggles to balance what she cannot balance in perpetuity. Our time has come to accept and understand what we are, the nature of this beautiful planet, and move ahead in accord and mutual respect and love to embrace a truly amazing and wonderful future; the implementation and achievement of a Plan for Earth at this time in her evolution that we have been working for consciously for many thousands of years.

The Light of Salvation

...is the creator's divine light of the universe. That is available to all mankind now. It has always been there but is now more visible, more accessible, than ever before. The clouds of negativity and darkness around Earth are clearing, opening up the pathway for truth, light, to pierce the bubble of illusion which has surrounded planet Earth for so long.

Rejoice, all of you. This is the time that you have all been working for through so many lifetimes. Let these words awaken those who are sleeping still so that they might respond and participate in the glorious new future for planet Earth before us. Blessings.

Ask for the light of the divine creator to come into you and flow through you. It will do so, setting you on a path to release, cleansing, purification, self-realisation and wellbeing, service, enlightenment and joy. Reach out and grasp your divine destiny now. It is time.

Waking Up to the Reality of Who We Are

This should be happening now to all on planet Earth, if it has not happened yet. Many here have been aware for years, decades even. A long hard road often as people's awareness grows incrementally as realisation dawns, frequently with haphazard moments of enlightenment along the way. Once a certain stage is achieved the soul actively looks for more information as the 'goal' falls into sight, the being understanding that there is ever more to know and that they stand at the beginning of a sacred journey into greater knowing, beyond all they had previously conceived.

All have sacred roles here on Earth at this time. All set plans into place before they came here, agreeing and knowing the time and circumstances at which they would awaken and consciously embrace and commence their role on planet Earth. I say consciously, as all have been working for this lifetime for many, many lifetimes before. All the learning, the lessons, are for the **now**, to help take humanity into the next step, the next stage, in its evolution. One of the greatest jobs in the universe!

That's our remit; what we have to undertake now to pull back planet Earth from the brink of disaster. What we have been seeing are the warning signs – which mankind has 'of course' ignored.

We have different roles. Our roles are unique to us individually. Some to heal, some to guide; teach others so that they can then develop and bring in the teaching of their own higher being, their soul, to show them what they need to do at this time. Some are to help with planetary healing; others to help the animals or plant kingdoms. Others to bring unity of people and purpose so that we can move forward into our new way of being on planet Earth.

The Magic of Love

*Love heals all. Love is the magic balm that has the power to cure all ailments, all suffering. Our hearts are at the very core of our being – they **are** our core – and along with love the light acts as a fuse which ignites the spark of being. Love and light work hand in hand throughout the universe.*

Redemption – that is the forgiveness through grace and actions of the highest good and discipline – comes when love and light blend in the psyche of the being and an awareness of a 'greater good', a higher, sacred requirement of our soul to touch the essence of God, comes into being.

When we love another person, another being, we set in motion, through that love essence, unlimited possibilities for expansion and knowing awareness. We set them free – or that love sets them free – to explore who and what they really are without fear of rejection or failure. They are truly empowered by that love. It gives them strength and courage and opens the way to unlimited growth and expansion. They truly may connect with God, the higher essence of which we are all part; the creator. For we are all one.

To love others is the most important action you can take at this time. Unconditional love is the purest form of love, which you are all recommended to seek and to develop within yourselves. It will take you, deliver you, to God, the all mighty being in this universe and all the universes.

The Dark Night of the Soul

This is an embryonic state, a state of awareness where one cannot see or find a way through to light and forward motion although the soul knows fully that the light is 'there' to be realised. There may be a fear of 'doing the wrong thing', taking incorrect actions.

In this state, stop and rest; pray frequently to the divine creator and ask for light to be downloaded into your being, your stellar gateway, that it might descend through you, even gradually. Know that your creator loves you so dearly, and ask to feel that great love. As the knowing of that love expands within you it will create cracks in the darkness, and the light will filter through.

When there is sufficient light you will be able to see the path into a new way, a new route to a different way of being. The first steps can be the most difficult. Follow your heart to the light.

Divine Focus

This is an awareness of the Divine coupled with the knowing that you need to make it your daily priority. That it is important above any other aspect of your life.

All things require balance but divine focus marshalls your energies and thoughts towards your daily actions and intention to raise your vibration ever upwards. To do what you can every day to increase your awareness and knowledge of the Divine and your part, your role, in developing your relationship with the Divine and your work here, your mission on Earth, as part of that divine focus. It is why you are here on planet Earth. Your divine reason for being (which is always divine).

There is nothing else in reality. All else is illusion. Do not be distracted by any illusion. You are divine. Focus on that knowledge and become the Divine. Be it.

Melancholy

Melancholy is a transient condition of the mind. It stems from frustration and anger – usually suppressed so that the individual does not even understand or suspect that they are angry at something. It could be this lifetime or in another in which the individual could not release negative feelings or emotions, and these have risen to the surface again in this incarnation. Often the person or persons contributing to the original causal situation are around them in this current lifetime (although this may not be evident to the individuals involved).

What to do?

From a healing perspective, bring in the light of the Holy Spirit and ask it to clear the conditions totally, or if this is not possible / is not working then ask to bring the situation or root of the melancholy to the surface, which will enable other modalities / processes to come into play by changing the dynamic. The violet flame is an excellent means to clear negativity and the person involved can be alerted to this method and empowered to use this themselves.

Melancholy can also arise from the inner frustration of awareness that one is not doing the work they came to this planet to undertake; they are not fulfilling their sacred mission. Again, the Holy Spirit and violet flame can help here to clear any blocks and to free up space for realisation to surface to consciousness. From this point the individual may take steps to move onto their correct pathway. Some changes will be conscious and some will come about without interference as the soul aligns itself, aided by guides and guardians. It is a beautiful process.

Sadness is not quite the same as melancholy as it usually has a specific known cause aligned to grief arising from loss or anticipated loss.

To help shift melancholy get out into the outdoors and bathe in the light – or bathe in the sea or water if you can. The light stimulates our bodies, our cells, and works on the cortex of the brain to send positive messages to our awareness. This enlivens our being and acts as a catalyst for more activity, positivity, and can help to engender a sense of useful purpose. Exercise can work in a similar fashion. Our bodies wake up and feel better, and the mind reacts and benefits.

A big aspect of healing is guiding people to tools they can use themselves to improve their positions and situations.

Melancholy is not the same as being in the void although someone may feel / experience melancholy as part of it. Melancholy can be aligned / associated with depression.

The Immortal Soul

Nothing ever dies, nothing is lost. All energy transmutes, changes in nature maybe, but is never extinguished totally. Our souls are like that. They persist beyond death, for life on this planet is currently characterised by a three dimensional body; flesh and blood and bone. It has needed to be that way in order to experience fully our third dimensional world. Our planet is however now changing, transforming herself into a fifth dimensional being, embracing a new glory and a new glorious environment; offering a new way to be for all sentient beings. We can all embrace what it means to become beings able to fully function in planet Earth's soon to be fifth dimensional reality.

Our individual transitions into the fifth dimension need to be conscious decisions, agreeing to this change. We can agree to this now, and initiate and instigate the necessary changes firstly by our intent to make the change, our willingness to move forwards into what is 'unknown' to most of us. I say 'unknown' because that is how it appears to be because of the veil of illusion, the veil that came down between our conscious self on this planet as we incarnated here, and our higher self, our immortal soul, which is expansive and knows what we are, our true, spectacular magnificence and majesty. We are all sovereign beings of love and light, and we chose, volunteered, to incarnate on planet Earth at this time in order to participate in and assist this glorious galactic event of planet Earth's – Gaia's – ascension from third dimension into the fifth dimension.

In the fifth dimension our lives will have no end until we desire it, until we reach a time when we feel we have learned and experienced all we can in that particular state and decide it is time for us to 'move on' to explore another situation, maybe a different planet, a different solar system, galaxy or universe even. That said, there is much work to do on planet Earth as our human collective transitions to the fifth dimension and establishes a new physical form, a new spiritual approach to living here. Things are going to be very different indeed.

Gone will be the greed, the envy, the distrust and suspicion which affects humankind's transactions – physical and energetic – on third dimensional Earth. In place will be communities of harmony, unity and love, where every one being is valued and considered as an equal participant in the whole... Is appreciated for what they bring to the collective for the collective. This is a society where every person is truly honoured for their individual gifts and talents. Where everyone peacefully and naturally accepts and owns their true status as a sovereign being who agrees to co-operate in a beautifully functioning society based on love and kindness and respect and trust. Where light illumines everything.

All natural light is divine light. *There is no other source of light. Light engenders all love.*

Light is the seed and source of everything. Without light there is nothing; there is the void. The void is the time to take a break, to pause, and to then move on into the light again.

The more light we hold individually, the better; the greater our capacity for love, for nurturing and nourishing ourselves and everyone around us. Light feeds and enhances. It can make us whole again. Hence the importance of light in healing. It uplifts us at a cellular level and enhances our bodies, mind, consciousness and emotions. It helps us to connect with our soul and thence our purpose. Light is everything.

Light empowers us, strengthens us, aligns us with what is good and right and pure. We can travel on light beams interstellarly. We can survive on light without food, and that is what sustains our light bodies, crystalline bodies. Fed with high vibrational light and love.

Healing in its widest sense: physical, mental, of emotion; expands our minds and consciousness and releases trauma and what we don't need in our being. It restores, releases those parts of us that are scattered, disparate, lost, and realigns the being into a beautiful whole soul. Light can do any and all of those things. Opens up our awareness to move forward into the 'new' future for us all.

At this stage, tell your body those changes are to come and that it should prepare itself for a magnificent shift which will allow it to process more light. As aforesaid, light enables more light. Bringing in light to your body is an early step in this magnificent process.

Choices We Make in Life

We make choices constantly. Some are minor and some are profound and can affect the ultimate way our lives unfold. All life is for learning.

A really important decision now is where our values lie. What is more important – planet Earth or our perceived wealth? Where do our hearts guide us? To the welfare of the animals and all natural life around us or to our pockets? Do we destroy the planet - so that it doesn't exist to support the life for all of our grandchildren - so that we can enjoy warmth, foreign holidays and an easier way of life that doesn't demand we focus our attention and have some difficult choices? We are at a crossroads.

Choose love. Love for the planet, the wildlife, people of all races, creeds, nations - that all may live on and enjoy a clean planet where food grows healthy and water flows clear. Where Earth's resources are shared fairly and not exploited. Where planet Earth and her rich offerings are respected, honoured and cherished.

Choosing love, honour and respect for ourselves is important, vital, too. Aligning ourselves with the righteous expands our being and allows more light to come through – which in turn expands our being and our sense of connection to the universe. We then are able to awaken to the great universal reality of what is really happening on this planet. The Great Awakening.

The soul's awakening

So how do you know your soul is awakening, and what do you do next? You start to see through the sham of what is apparently around you. You may question what you are being told / asked to do by certain organisations and society around you. There is a groundswell now of community consciousness that is swiftly underpinning the realities of love and the want to ensure wellbeing for all members of our society. For some they become suddenly aware of a sense of 'greater purpose' – a reason why they are here and the role they have accepted; their 'mission'.

The Whispers of Youth

Youth offers many gifts: vitality, suppleness, power, radiance if we are fortunate and in good health. Also a clear mind – a clean slate in some ways.

If we are nurtured by our parents we are free of responsibilities which may impinge on our beliefs, our ideals of what we would like to incorporate into our futures. We most often choose our parents; the family and circumstances we wish to incarnate into, so that we have a good start – the best opportunity to ensure that we are able to complete the mission we have for that particular incarnation on planet Earth. [Note that a 'good start' to enable success in our mission may not necessarily be a comfortable or easy start!]

Now, with Covid impacting the schooling and education systems around the world, there are even greater opportunities for young people, young minds, to grow and develop without the 'imprint', the interference of the societal belief systems and values of their elders which in many cases have sadly been warped by the need to 'survive' and gain financial strength. That security is an illusion. The young people, the souls being born now, know this instinctively and also know that they have come here for a very different purpose with the intention, the need, to change fundamentally how our societies have been operating on Earth for the past few centuries. The loss of formal education in many ways simply helps to free them from 'knowledge' that they may not need, and which can only hinder them in some instances.

All is working perfectly, going as it should. Have faith and trust.

The curious circumstances of present times feed the minds and attitudes of those who have come here specifically to change things. The status quo has been upset totally and will be forced out. It is time. It has begun, and begun so wonderfully.

The Flower of Life

The Flower of Life is indeed the key to, the summation of, all things in the universe. It holds every-thing, if you can only see and understand it. It weaves its mystery for those who can see to unlock.

When used in conjunction with what are called the axiatonal lines it enables a new, fresh – or should we say – refreshed connection with all life. The axiatonal lines emanate from the intersections, the nexus points, when the divine process is activated. This enables a series of events to unfold for the being in question. It's like being plugged back in to the electricity supply, except much, much more elaborate and sophisticated, and far more powerful. It is all-expanding. It offers keys to so many different, newly 'heard of', aspects of the universe that will take mankind to a totally new way of interacting with the rest of the universe, of being, and of becoming 'whole'. It is a healing process, a new modality if you like, but it is also so much more than this.

The axiatonal lines which emanate from and surround the body are like tethers. At the moment they [most usually] tether to nothing. They are like electrical connections which plug into nothing, and the end connection is no longer the 'right fit' for the system it needs to plug into. The system has become obsolete because it has not been used. It has not been used largely because the connections were cut – ie mankind was disconnected – thousands of years ago (before the fall of Atlantis). It is time to plug back into the universal matrix. This will lead to many wonderful things for us now on planet Earth. Amazing possibilities.

Behind the scenes things are being switched on again for planet Earth. This will enable new useful connections to be made that are powerful and transformative. This will enable access to new understanding, new approaches to healing mental and physical issues; new capabilities that we can barely comprehend. We are being brought back on line! Will be revolutionary! Children coming in now are activated physically for these processes to run effectively and efficiently; for the energy to connect and fully flow.

Water is a superconductor. No coincidence that Earth is a watery planet. To take advantage of the new incoming possibilities we need to individually drink a lot more water daily than most of us do.

The Flower of Life

It is a peaceful time. *It may not look like that, however.*

The giants of the cosmos are all around, watching and waiting for mankind to emerge from darkness.

It is a joyful time. It may not look like that now.

You on planet Earth are what you choose to be at any time. You choose your reality by creating it, through your thoughts, your actions, day to day. Choose love for others, and peace will follow. Choose love for yourself and those around you - all beings around you - and joy will follow.

As you think, so you will become. It is a law of the universe. Be the love you wish to see.

We all Heal Ourselves Ultimately

On planet Earth at this time this healing largely comes hand in hand with remembering who we are and waking up to our self-power, our sovereignty as a human being and as a wise entity of the cosmos. We are all beings of light, part of the great Source, the God, that lives at the heart of all knowing and all consciousness. We are all part of that supreme being of light.

When we accept this as truth we start to unravel the tangle of confusion, doubt, misunderstanding, misconceptions and wrong beliefs that beset mankind at this time. Healing comes from within us for ourselves. It can be a long process, and it can be a quick process. What is important is that we embark upon this path and free ourselves to become part of the light force.

These are difficult times on planet Earth. They are also wondrous times. A time of great glory is very close. The universe, the multiverse even, is watching as mankind makes its way out of the darkness into the light. The light of knowing, understanding and love. Humankind knowing who they are, understanding where they came from and how and why they are on planet Earth, and embracing the truth of their historical purpose here and their roles now and in the future.

Now is a time of glorious change for all – the planet and her people. It is time for all to embrace love, and unity, and move forward together. It is a time for joy.

Goodness comes from the heart, *when all is said and done. A greatness, a capacity to love, to feel, to honour and to hold fast to what we know is true. We are all being tested in this way now. Asked to be true to ourselves and our fundamental beliefs about what is right and wrong in this world. To stand by our principles and the guidelines that we set for ourselves, often subconsciously, in this world.*

*Those who adhere to their fundamental beliefs and principles and stand firm are blessed. Of course it is required that those fundamental principles are of the light, borne in a love for ourselves and those around us, our neighbours. A love for all mankind and an inner quest, knowing, that all are equally important in the eyes of God and all due respect for **their** beliefs and principles where these are aligned with good, with love and a pure heart.*

Listen to what your heart tells you and let it be your guide in all things. Blessed one. You are all blessed ones.

The beauty of planet Earth is unsurpassed. *The gardens, the vegetation, the lush growth of so many varied life forms. You are truly blessed on planet Earth. Too bad that mankind does not fully appreciate the great and beautiful abundance of its surroundings and setting.*

Beauty takes many forms and is of course subjective. We know this in our own environment, the environment of the knowing ones, those who inhabit those realms, those dimensions, where we actively create our surroundings, our environment, from moment to moment if we so wish.

Mankind is learning the lessons that will enable it to manage the creation of his / her environment in a responsible way too. We all create our own reality, in truth. You have the beautiful setting of planet Earth and yet many of you create pain, hurt, abandonment – an ugly society for your souls, your selves.

Learn that the beauty around you can be reflected in the beauty within you if you so wish. Look for the light and love around you and breathe it into your being, your physical being, daily. The essence of that beauty will fill you, if you allow it to do so, and uplift you so that you become part of the beauty of this wonderful, vibrant, lush, bountiful planet Earth. She is to be safeguarded.

The Positioning of the Light

Light has / holds many facets not yet all known to mankind. What you know and understand is the tip of the iceberg, as you would say. Light will gift mankind - indeed gifts all beings in this great multiverse - with many, many wonderful attributes and possibilities – for healing, for creating, for manifesting, for being. It is the raw material of the universe. Light is everywhere. Even the darkness is an aspect of light, as many of you will know.

Light has energy, is energy, and will offer and provide a route – one of many new routes and pathways – out of planet Earth's current troubles. Within you all is the awareness, understanding, of the great possibilities of light in this planetary context and you will quickly wake up to and work with its many, beautiful aspects with ease and alacrity as you 'remember'.

Light technology is coming to planet Earth. It is here already and now it will be discovered, or uncovered, and brought in to the main stream of possibilities for solutions now - in all sorts of ways and aspects. Healers have been aware of the uses of light for many, many years and have harnessed some of its possibilities in consciously allowing / bringing in the light to flow through them. This is going to shift into a whole new game on a much higher level.

We will truly live in the light, using our conscious awareness of light in a far wider aspect in order to create, modify and enhance our lives and also the impact of our lives here on planet Earth. It is a glorious time ahead. And it is, as your media like to emphasise, Coming Soon!!! (Although of course it is actually here already!)

Love and blessings, Archangel Metatron.

Robots of the Light

These are small light forms which will assist mankind in cleaning up planetary waste, such as plastics. They will be able to operate in many environments where there are polluting substances which are micro-based, eg microorganisms and microplastics. They work by ingestion and will be operated by light – even at huge depths in the ocean. There are slightly different forms for different environments but will be borne of the same idea, compounds, and operated / programmed by light and crystal.

Deep ocean, surface water environments, land; air (although this will not be the most differentiated since light moves easily through this material / substance, if you like), the body even - this will be one of the most useful arenas for this light technology. Programmed by thought and intention.

Just as thought propels space travel capsules in terms of direction (or rather, should we say, destination and speed / time of arrival) then will these medical packets of light intention be delivered, steered, conducted through the body to their required 'ports of call'. Healers bring light through the body already and the greater awareness and understanding of the capacities of light – and its availability to the third dimension towards healing for the fifth dimensional environment - will enable greater things. A bit like miniature light drones. Focus is required.

Cloud technology

These light drones will be able to saturate the clouds and be distributed in these ways, but also through thought and intention. We are all so excited here!

Right now, light tends to degrade plastic – change its composition - but it does not eradicate it. With new manipulations of light, this light will be able to alter the base compound and render it susceptible to light destruction techniques that will in turn then render it harmless – I can see it melting and being washed away as a harmless compound that is absorbed into the natural elements; air, fire, water, earth. These elementals will play their parts too!

All sentient life forms on planet Earth are marshalling and getting prepared for the assault to assuage the damage, the havoc, that has and is being wrought on planet Earth. Humanity is waking up to the new way of being. The elementals here are aware and are also actively preparing to take on their active roles at this time, working hand in hand with the angelic realms and light beings and with mankind as we quickly evolve at this time and our awareness grows exponentially.

Beautiful beings of planet Earth; *knowing ones in this existence. Your time on planet Earth has come to fruition. This is a time of splendour, joy and great welcoming of the energies of beings across the universe, the multiverse even. Some of you are perceiving the change of tone on your planet. Don't be misled by the tribulations mankind is undergoing. These are necessary in order to catalyse the events and changes that must take place. Mankind is moving into the final stage of a grand transition, and God's Will on Earth will be done.*

The light coming into your planet – its light quotient - is increasing daily now and the power of that light is cleansing, clearing and opening up new opportunities for all. Breathe in the light consciously and ask it to suffuse your physical being and the energy body that surrounds it. It will uplift you and release negativity and fear, and enable you to interact with your fellow beings, family and neighbours on a more positive level. As you do this you grow and expand.

From small beginnings come many beautiful things, many beautiful beings. The light heals.

There are so many aspects to what is happening now on planet Earth. *It is a major operation on a galactic, a universal level even, and so very many light beings and light collective from the angelic, galactic and cosmic realms are participating. As word carries regarding what is happening on your planet – the undertaking, and the speed of progress - other beings from farther realms of the universe, the multiverse (for this is not the only universe) are being drawn to take a look and, in some cases, to offer and add their help, their energies, to this great, magnificent undertaking.*

You are all such special beings on Earth. Brave, masterful and yet most of you still have no idea of this. You are volunteers of the rarest kind, called from the universe to be on planet Earth at this time – in some cases for millennia here, in Atlantis, and even prior to that.

Clearly planet Earth is in great trouble at this time but we can help with this. What is occurring on planet Earth goes beyond the planetary destruction. It has been part of a cosmic experiment involving free will of mankind, and the results from this, the fallout, have been far-reaching. Light beings are amassing around your world to help pull things through, and it will be done.

Be joyful. Focus your attention on the wonderful things around you. On the beauty this planet offers, the glory of the sunrise and sunset, the joy of warmth, the breeze, the refreshment of the seas, the wonder of the natural world. On the kindness of people around you, the smiles, the laughter, the small kindnesses. Acknowledge these things and look for them. Find this wonder and joy where ever you can, and thus you will amplify them not just for yourself but for your fellow human beings, because that is the nature of these things.

The acknowledgment, the understanding, the process of looking for - seeking out - the positives is infectious. Spread joy, laughter, kindness and love.

The source of light is a microcosm in the universe. *We are all bathed in this beautiful light which emanates from it. This light is elastic and wraps itself around things. Aspects of it run through solid objects as variations in the form of light. You may ask, what then is light?*

Light entraps molecules, certain parts of living things, which can cause harm or detriment, or change the condition of the object (thing or person). It deals with these molecules according to a set of codes and conditions which are set and regulated by those in the highest dimensions. The nature of light is therefore not necessarily constant, although it is constant until a being of the highest order, Source, decides that an aspect needs to change or be modified. This is not a regular occurrence.

Light cleanses and clears. It also shows the shadow (non-light) aspect of people, objects and the environment, and the non-physical aspects because, as you may be aware, physicality and non-physicality are subjective and depend upon circumstances and perception.

How can the shadow side of a non-physical entity be processed? We perceive it with our non-physical senses, often through the senses and intelligences we engage with through our third eye − that door of perception that takes us into a very different world − The Real World that we all inhabit rather than the third dimensional world.

It is only when we start to look at and sense what is around us and 'there' with our third eye that we truly begin to 'see'. And what we see is subtle and may be subjective depending upon how good our third eye 'sight' is and how trained, how exercised, our senses are. Third eye vision is linked to substances in our brain and the way that our nervous system operates in connection and communication with them, and their interaction with the pineal gland.

The pineal gland can calcify in the modern world because of the way many of us live; our diet, awareness and so on. The violet flame can help to enhance and revive the pineal gland. It can burn away the calcification and unwanted residues that often surround this tissue and cloud its potentially clear, sharp perceptions. This is one of the most useful aspects of the violet flame at this time. You can also bring in golden light (I [Metatron] am seeing pale yellow gold) to clean the lens, so to speak, of the third eye. The clearer the lens becomes the more light can get to the lens, so it is self-expanding in that way.

You may hear adepts and those connected with higher knowledge speak about the 'veils of amnesia'. This is but one aspect of clear sight (clairvoyance literally) and the associated clarities that third eye clearing can reveal. Polishing the lens through the use of tools such as violet flame, and clearing any specks, dust, that have arisen within, are further steps that can be taken to clear, to hone, your third eye clarity once the veils have been lifted. For many that is just an initial step.

*And what about the fourth eye and the fifth eye? All energy points in your energetic being that work to enhance your perceptions when they are ready which, of course, is when **you** are ready. Eventually that whole area of the metaphysical body merges with your crown. At that point you can start to think about, consider, teleportation, also higher aspects of healing.*

Provided that your intent is pure you are limited in your power and ability only by what you can imagine is possible. You are so blessed! But of course once you awaken to what you really are and the potential (unlimited!) of yourself as a being who works only with the light you realise that every single aspect of life, every source of life in this universe, is an aspect of Source – the great divine Source – and therefore we are all blessed – angels, archangels, ascended masters, galactic light beings. We all have magnificent powers. The issue on Earth is that most of you haven't a clue - just don't realise it. Fortunately this is now changing. Welcome to the light!

Send light to all around you; white light, pure light, with pure intention.

The colours of light determine / indicate the vibrational level of the light you are dealing with, accessing, or really it can be considered vice-versa.

Black holds all colours as you may know. The vibrational levels have different effects on a person's body or an object, on energy itself, depending upon circumstances. It is also a reason why intention is so important in our approach to how we utilise light, for example, and one reason why it can be so powerful and often advisable to allow the angels and other higher realms to determine exactly what is to be sent where. They can see and comprehend the finer detail and provide exactly what is needed at any one specific time. No light is 'bad' but there may be better, more appropriate, colours or qualities of light to use than others in the same set of circumstances.

There are general guidelines of course. We think of green as a healing colour; white and gold too. Orange for energy. Blue for calm. Mauve for clearing. But it can become very complex indeed. The 'right ' colour can be a different colour in any set of circumstances. Important therefore when healing to ask for higher guidance – and indeed to be connected with your higher self at all times so that you are connected to the highest source of information that you can access. And then you need to trust.

Golden light has a different hue to white light and a different purpose; different attributes, capabilities and potentials. It is softer, gentler, than pure white light and more likely to offer warmth, love and comfort; feelings of security. It builds and pulls together, unifies rather than 'cuts through'. It is the light of the angels; realising that all is well. A feeling of ambience and wellbeing. These attributes can be created in a person, an organ, a situation, around fear, worry.

It creates harmony, and all is well. It softens rigidity and dispels cacophonous situations, jagged environments, contrariness, disjoint and disorder, sharp edges. Gold is eleventh dimensional energy.

Pure white light holds a sharp edge. It cuts, clears and expels. It is loving energy but more clinical and disinfecting than golden light. It acts to expose truth and dissolves falsehood and false appearances, in any situation. It excises anything that is no longer wanted / required. It reduces fuzziness and weight and therefore uplifts – literally enables a situation, person or energetic aspect of something or someone – whatever it is applied to – to rise up because it is lighter, no longer weighed down by denser energies. It is an application of – or respects - physics.

Blue light cools and calms. It takes heat, or unwanted heat and warmth, out of a situation, or tissue, or person and thus allows other aspects of light to work more in keeping with their own characteristics and potentials. Blue light can heal trauma – physical or mental. It reduces swelling or energetic expansion due to heightened emotions or situations. Blue calms. The 'hotter' aspects of a situation can no longer remain attached with this cooling and they naturally detach and drift away; they are no longer tethered to the situation. They dispel / transmute. Blue refreshes – our bodies, our minds and our emotions. It's like a reset.

Orange dispels gloom and enhances energy in all aspects of thought, activity; speeds up processes in the body and therefore revitalises. It has a disinfecting approach also, cleansing and clearing lower moods and sluggishness in all respects - again - people, organs, mental, physical, environmental. It's like an injection of the wish to be 'active' – of body, mind, creativity. Like a spark, a charge. Orange banishes *lethargy. It's like a tonic wherever it is used. Archangel Metatron's favourite colour!*

Red *emboldens and strikes. It says, 'I am here' – which is why it was the standard grounding colour. Telling the planet, reminding the planet, that we are here and ready for action. Red is heat, which can be useful at times to speed up a process when there is little life, but must be used with care. It can destroy but it does not have the intelligence of the mauve / purple ray which also destroys and removes, but brings in blue and pink to 'modify' and 'mediate' the rawness of red. Red rushes in. Therefore exercise caution and guidance at every single occasion before use.*

Rainbow light's *beauty and power is that it brings in all the different colours and hues. Everything is there so all possibilities, all 'posts', if you like, are covered. Just let the rainbow light do its work intelligently.*

Rainbow light links the beholder to the heavens. *A rainbow never ceases to inspire delight, attention of the very heart. Uplifting, and a symbol of hope and joy. The colour, the quality of the aspect, is a wonder, a joy, of the universe. The quality of the rainbow is very special.*

Remember the Rainbow Warriors and the tale, the legend, that is handed down by the Native American Indians, of hope, of a passing of the suppression of modern times. The fruition of this legend, the end-story, is unfolding now. A time of joy, anticipation and excitement. Those of you on Earth who are waking up to this awareness of the enormity of what is unfolding now on planet Earth share this expectation even if you are not quite sure what is happening. It's because you know within your self, your higher self, the massive, wonderful events of this time and the promise of the future that is in store for us, magnificent beyond our current comprehension.

*There exist in the universe colours that we cannot yet recognise on third dimensional planet Earth. Sound invokes colour, sometimes images, in our mind. It is why some people listen to music in a different way. Sound connects with each of us in individual ways - just as we are individuals, and reflecting our unique make-up - and invokes different things in all of us, because we **are** unique.*

The power of light is unsurpassed. *Light beings in many parts of the universe dedicate themselves to understanding light and developing wonderful techniques which utilise its power and its properties. They combine these facets of light with their own particular capabilities and the characteristics of the environment in which they are serving to develop amazing and wonderful capacities.*

New and wonderful uses of light that you have not yet seen in action or practice on planet Earth will soon be utilised on this planet to help to allay some of the problems you have created and allowed to develop in your environment. Mankind's inability to recognise and understand planet Earth as a holistic being whose parts are co-dependent, and work as one symbiotic being, have allowed, encouraged, the component parts to stop working together, causing the breakdown of the structural unity and the collapse of planet Earth's ecosystems.

Planet Earth is the blue jewel of the universe and will not be allowed to disintegrate further.

The light that emanates through a crystal is amplified. The properties of the crystal expand the light refraction and it gives the light different capacities and capabilities largely depending upon the type and colour – and quality – of the crystal. That is why crystals used in precision machinery are generally manufactured so that no inflexions or faults are present that might affect the accuracy of the crystal's function and effectiveness, ie through introducing errors and mistakes into the process.

The colour of the crystal can affect the outcome, the quality and attributes of the light as it refracts. All crystals have power and energy (should we say the energy comes first) but those which are clear quartz-based are the most powerful as they have a clarity, a perspicacity, which intensifies the beam of light. The colour of the crystal enhances the power of that colour in its various uses. It's like a generator or amplifier. When the universal intention is added to a crystal, ie through the intention of the healer or the person using it, its capacity, its power, increases manifold accordingly.

You have heard of 'the rays'. The rays, which are described by light, their colour, are overseen by masters who govern and monitor their capacities and are sometimes asked to add an aspect to the colour ray under their guardianship when it is time for a new characteristic, a new attribute, to be introduced to this planet.

There were once seven rays but there will be more; more coming into play as mankind develops and it becomes possible, indeed desirable and necessary even, to add a layer of new information and possibilities; a complexity, to the pattern of colour function on planet Earth.

The violet ray, for example, is multiplying its aspects to assist the cleansing and clearing required here on Earth. Violet flame, silver violet flame, platinum violet flame, lilac fire... There are many variations and each has its own niche attributes and uses although in a general way they all help to cleanse and clear.

This variation, this fine tuning, is going to happen with other colours soon. Maybe yellow is next as it is close to gold and pales to almost white; so is important in that respect. Yellow informs and provides enlightenment of obscure or hidden information and will enable mankind to see with more depth, clarity and detail things that were previously hidden, ie knowledge will appear into the light as the light qualities at our disposal on planet Earth will increase and expand.

Our sun has an orange-yellow light which is no accident at this time. It is perfect in which to bathe for both upliftment, reassurance and to enable us to grow into our fifth dimensional bodies and roles and environment here. But the nature of our sun will also change at some point. Also, as you know, the main source of spiritual light to this planet has recently changed, from the great central sun of the universe to the light of the seven sacred suns of this and near galaxies. This is a reflection of our growing requirement and our capacity to bring in more detailed, distinct and defined light qualities to help and enable us to develop finer tuning and higher definition of aspects of our souls' abilities and openness to information and knowledge and awareness - to enable and reflect, mirror, our growth. All is in perfect timing.

The beauty we perceive in those lights, those objects that can enable and expand our growth, is no accident. Take, for example, a shell on the beach that holds a veneer of mother-of-pearl over even one side, on one plane, even a small area. It shines in the light - particularly sunlight which enhances of course - and the mother-of-pearl glints and reflects a rainbow of colour. We are attracted by that light, the glint and gleam and beauty of the colours, and its shine. We may pick up to examine more closely... We may marvel at its beauty, the colour it refracts. At that point we are connected to the universe as we are momentarily transported into a place where the beauty of the shell is our focus. All else drops away, albeit temporarily. For that moment we have been taken into a different place, a different dimension even.

That is the power, the gift, of beauty that is all around us. Shells, flowers, birds, insects, dawn, a sunset. All part of God. All to bring us close to the Divine and our divine roots, our divine selves.

Light Essences, Keys and Codes

The light of the seven suns shines brightly over planet Earth at this time. It feeds in light essences that are required for the transformation, the stepping up, acceleration, promotion of your lives on planet Earth into the fifth dimension.

Do not doubt – this will happen very soon in your Earth years. The process is under way and will not be stopped. These light essences provide attributes and propensities that feed mankind with the information and the will to undertake the changes that are required. The light uplifts and also cleanses, and that cleansing can disrupt and create discomfort for people – growth is not always comfortable, so it may not look or feel uplifting at all times. This applies to planet Earth just as much as to her peoples. It is a time of huge joy and celebration as planet Earth and her populations expand their consciousness and move into ever higher levels of light but it is also a very bumpy ride at the same time.

Trust. Draw light into your being daily and see it, visualise it, running down from above the top of your head through your body and your legs down into the earth, the centre of the Earth. The light flows from the heavens and reinforces your connection to planet Earth. Thus you are connected, heaven to Earth. It is good.

The facets of the light from the seven galactic suns are diverse and important. Be aware that they are awakening within humans, at this time, pre-programmed codes of light which reside dormant within you all from your birth. When the light touches an aspect of you at the right time, so to say, it awakens that code, that seed of knowing, and sets a reaction in you that will propel you forward. It is quite wonderful. The combination of the suns' lights and your receptive bodies awaken a propensity to greater understanding of what is happening around you and this understanding in itself – separate from all other influences of the light and code interaction – stabilises individuals and how they relate to and react to events on planet Earth at this time, for much is happening, in case you hadn't noticed! (laughs).

It is not just the suns' light which awakens these innate, inert codes. Other interactions can do this too, and codes can also be downloaded into our selves at other times from other sources. Mankind is a truly wonderful, complex being! They are codes of love and light and magnificence designed to lighten and uplift. They are pure.

Animals and elementals too perceive and receive these lights and codes. We are all interacting in a wonderful and complex matrix. It is a matrix predominantly of love and light, although other aspects can surface at this time. Light codes are being awoken throughout the natural world, in plants, birds and in the planet of Earth too. Earth has been part of an experiment in the universe and it is time now for this to end and for things to change. We are here to help that process transition. The move into the fifth dimension runs as part of this transition to a different way of being on planet Earth.

*Promoting love is the only way to encourage mankind away from fear and encourage all to take those necessary steps. It **is** the plan for planet Earth therefore.*

The pink light is an unusual one in that it is a light of love but it also unsettles those who are not focused on love, who are not coming from a place of love. It repels them, and they find the light repellent. It is an interesting vibration.

Normally, sending love induces feelings of wellbeing and reciprocation in the one receiving the love. Love in these cases where the 'receiving' person is actively, almost consciously and deliberately, acting in a way that is not loving creates significant difficulties. Pink light is a good way to get someone, a darker energy, to move away. It will not necessarily clear that darker, heavier energy, but it will move to a distance away.

Pink is the light of Archangel Chamuel, the archangel governing the heart space and its many aspects. Pink is the colour of love but also of nurturing. It is a soft love, reflecting the pink hue; compassion and understanding, an unconditional love. This loving aspect unsettles those who do not share that deep sense of loving others because it links to an aspect of them that reminds them on a deep level that they are lacking an aspect of love that they should rightfully hold, own and exhibit. It exposes a shortcoming in them and they recognise this at a deep level. That is why they retreat from the situation.

Some affected in this way will re-examine themselves and feel prompted to amend their behaviour. Others will just move away and on to a situation elsewhere that does not stimulate their discomfort, ie focus on a being or situation that does not respond to them in a loving way that disturbs them, ie that they find disturbing.

Purple imbues a sense of importance. *It is also a cleanser as it can absorb all other colours and hues that emanate and hold a vibration of darkness that is not of the light. It is like sponge for negativity. Its other attributes clear that darkness and dispel it, transmuting it so that it is no longer so heavy and can be separated and cleared.*

Its use as a colour to represent power and regality comes from the knowledge that it would cleanse and clear those who wore it and help to purify and keep cleansed the objects that one holds sacred or symbolise the power, the authority, to be recognised.

It is a most versatile colour, its hues extending from softest lilac to deepest rich purple. It absorbs all other qualities and aspects of light and absorbs and reflects, in this way, love, joy, responsibility and solemnity. Its importance in healing comes from its propensity to clear negativity and darkness. It also is like a seed for purity, the magenta being the solid foundation for new beginnings and new aspirations.

Use the violet flame everywhere on planet Earth now. She needs this hue to help her pull through these times. Sending the violet flame, and the love of the gold and the energy and unity of orange, will do much to help.

Yellow is colour, a vibration, that enriches. *The yellow ray brings about joy, uplifts, also bestows information and awareness. Essentially it allows a greater flow of perceptions, information and knowledge to be achieved, and therefore an expanded view. It allows us to see into the greater detail therefore and enables us to undertake more, and gifts us with more enlightenment. It reveals the joy in all things since all that is not of the dark holds joy. Therefore if there is joy we perceive that joy that comes through as understanding and appreciation of the greater details, the finer aspects.*

Enlightenment means seeing things in a perspective offered by greater light and it is the greater light that allows us to see beyond the obvious. That will be a big part of the gift of fifth dimensional living; being able to see, appreciate and understand the finer aspects of all things. Acknowledging and becoming aware of more opens us up to greater awareness and understanding and so our ability to understand becomes deeper and wider and, like a sponge, we absorb more and more of the new knowledge.

How do We Move into the Fifth Dimension?

Things are changing rapidly on planet Earth. Archangel Metatron has said that the ways in which people might access 'their' fifth dimensional space will change over time. Some are likely to be already using a process as part of their daily spiritual practice to consciously move their focus into a higher vibrational dimension. For those seeking guidance Metatron has offered the following as possible considerations towards moving forward: (Remember that you have his protection; see How to Use this Document, page 9.)

We consciously allocate, visualise, create, an energetic space - possibly above our stellar gateway chakra - which we identify as our individual fifth dimensional realm.

What we see, and what we think of, does bring about a perceptible change in our heads. It's a physical sensation which is a reflection of what we are looking at. One reason why what we think and hold in our thoughts is so important is that it shapes our reality. So, we identify a place that is our fifth dimensional space, and we sit quietly, bring down the light, and then we 'go to' our fifth dimensional place. We see what is there; we take a look. As we breathe we can bring in light to that fifth dimensional area. We may visualise a fifth dimensional world that is beautiful, clear of pollution, bright, sparkling, cleansed, clear and uplifted. Music can help us to find that fifth dimensional space. You may find your vibration changing as you access that place – feel a tingling sensation in your head, third eye possibly.

Knowing your fifth dimensional place and knowing your route to accessing it is important and will become even more so as time goes on. Planet Earth herself is moving up and you need to have your *awareness, your being, installed in that area, that dimension of reality – for it **is** reality – and it will become your new daily reality.*

*Look for those things you wish to become part of that fifth dimensional reality, acknowledge them – the love, unity of all people, joy, kindness, sharing, help to those around you; acknowledge as you see it as something that you wish for in the fifth dimension, to be a part of that consciousness. That helps to ground that aspect into your reality. Look for and see that which you wish to be your experience in the new way of being. Reinforce it in this way. Be the person you wish to be. Just **be** it. Kindness, love, compassion, understanding, forgiveness, calm, fortitude, strength, support to others. We have opportunities to display these every day even if it is just going outside and extending a smile to another being. Or meditating, or thinking about those less fortunate and maybe placing them in a shower of light from the heavens. Let us be our fifth dimensional selves.*

Ignore as many aspects of the third dimension as you can; the news, the day to day that pulls you into this existence rather than the higher realms.

You may wish to use the violet flame / violet fire to cleanse and clear our environment and the planet. Or to sit quietly, focus your thoughts, and [for example] *imagine rain clouds amassing over those places where the heat is intense; bring down the rain and see the land cooling off.*

As you think so you become. Our thoughts are so powerful. Thought runs the universe. It is the operating system! All is thought. Use your mind now to create your fifth dimensional 'planet'; your new existence here on planet Earth. Other things are happening too but your thoughts, your thinking, is a huge component in what we will collectively create here.

Thought runs the universe. From travel speeds to the light ships that consciousness travels in, we create largely with our minds. On third dimensional Earth you have third dimensional creations, an awful lot of work and effort. Creating with our minds is relatively effortless when you know how and get into the swing of it, ie practise! When you are working collectively the combined thoughts are so very powerful.

One 'problem', if you like, on planet Earth has been that the intent, the fundamental, of the third dimension that you all have free will, has grown a cult of individuality. 'Everyone wants to be different' and to display that individuality for all to see: 'I Am Different!' Now is the time for us to be our selves, our divine selves. Not to say that we cannot be what is comfortable; if that is different that is fine provided that it does not compromise another being's freedom to be what they are. It is also time for us to work for the planet; that is largely why we are here.

*The way in which we think, how we exercise our capacity to think and create through thought - create our realities, individually and collectively - will underpin our ability to rescue this planet; to help her move forwards / upwards in her personal ascension into the new dimension. She will change, with our without us. We can help her, and we can change things. We just need to **do it now**. The floods, the fires, have shown us this.*

The numbers are up now for so many species on Earth. It was anticipated, and they know and understand and even look forward to returning to their home planets, but even so there is sadness. Sadness mostly for mankind who has not yet risen to the challenge of putting its house truly in order on planet Earth. Money overrides everything, it seems. And greed may not [must not] end human life on Earth.

The crossroads is here. It is more like a T-junction. Go one way and it is peril and loss. The other is difficult but is survival. Fear of the unknown stops man making the 'right' decisions. Fear of loss of income, of the resources to keep things going. Some are genuine in their concern that if we do things differently they will not be able to sustain livelihoods of themselves and their employees; but mind if it comes from greed and disdain of life and the bountiful offerings of this planet. So the animals and species are sad. They go home in accord but leave the beauty this wonderful planet offers to all.

How then do we make this change in the minds of men? The longer it is left the more difficult to make the change. Action under duress is not so easy when the choices are fewer and the land is burning. Burning is a cleansing process and the people will literally burn with it, as a plague burns, or is deliberately burnt to cleanse. Be aware. Man has become a plague on the face of the Earth.

Collective action can be used to help slow down or remedy and limit the reaction of planet Earth to the pressures she is under; to bring in rain to cool and wet the land to stop the fires. Shifting the weather patterns just sends heat to other places that cannot assimilate it. The heat response needs to be ameliorated.

Use the violet flame.
Talk to planet Earth.
Heed the warnings and act now.

We are all here for a purpose. *A fundamental purpose that may be reflected in our aspirations. Or it could be something far less obvious. A requirement, agreement, to take away negativity when we depart this planet. All have purpose.*

Purpose is what motivates individuals. It enables us to apply a form to our life, a shape, a framework in which to fit those higher actions and activities – which are going to enable us to move towards achieving our purpose. Some purposes are daily and routine and others more major – to study and apply ourselves so that we can do the things in life that we enjoy – whether that is our work, filling our leisure time, or fulfilling our esoteric or spiritual purpose here.

For many, their purposes are hidden until the time is right. For many the time is right now to discover the spiritual purpose of our existence here. In our higher selves, in our hearts, we hold that information. We need to unlock it so that we can realise / release it and set to work either undertaking it or taking the steps towards doing it, if it is something that requires our preparation or training.

Go into your heart and ask for the information to be revealed to you. Without purpose we are like ships at sea, tossed in the waves and by the wind. We need a rudder to take us to our destination. It is an old analogy but an appropriate one. We all need rudders at this time. That, and a purpose. There are so many distractions. Equally there is much on this planet that needs to be done, even if you are not yet sure it is your 'life's purpose'. Helping your community, befriending a neighbour, growing your own food, reviewing and improving your diet, consciously assessing how our actions can help the planetary pollution and environmental stresses. Learning a healing technique so that we can assist others. Taking responsibility to empower ourselves so that we in turn can empower others.

There are many useful purposes and actions we can undertake while we await the revelation of our divine purpose here.

We may find our divine purpose by becoming quiet, looking inwardly in meditation, and asking our hearts - 'What is our heart's desire?' [Or] by raising our vibration and going upwards into a higher place to find the answers (ask our higher selves). Our purpose will give us joy, or the prospect of joy. Our life and work here on planet Earth should be joyful.

The Purpose of Life on Earth for Mankind

Clearly there is much happening on planet Earth at this time and most of you think in terms of raising your vibration and clearing up the planet. Of course this must be done. Both are critical and indeed complement each other. There are other factors in play here, however.

Just as there is a collection of enlightened and high vibrational beings assisting planet Earth at this time so is there a collective on Earth, ie mankind is a collective of beings of light and joyful willing beings of love from across the universe who agreed to come here and help on planet Earth. Some of you have been here for many, many incarnations, perpetually held in unawareness while in each of the great roles you have willingly undertaken to help at this time. At some point you will be given the opportunity to return to your homes – your original planets. Soldiers returning from active service, if you like.

You will take with you so much experience and knowing that will help other planets and life forms to move ahead in so many ways. You have brought your loving intent to planet Earth at this time, or over these times, and you will return to your home planet with so many gifts – a wealth of information and experience and knowing. You are part of a great force of light.

The wonders, the achievement, that is about to unfold on planet Earth will be applauded across the cosmos. You will have new roles therefore if you wish, using your knowledge and experience gained. It will not be dull. There will be a period of readjustment; that is natural. And rest too for those who require it. Blessed ones. You are beloved.

The Gifts of the Light

Light arouses love, healing, upliftment, cleansing and clearing, joy and purification for all beings that it touches. It also changes the nature of solid objects (although in reality there is no such thing as a solid object – just an apparent solid object!) Light changes everything. It is the foundation of all things and all things respond to changes in the quality of light.

Light carries keys and codes which initiate changes in the recipient or receiving material. Light carries knowledge and information. Bathe and bask in it so as to amplify and expand your own awareness and perceptions. Close your eyes and bring in universal light and give yourselves a light bath of the highest order. Bring in the light of the moon, the sun and the sacred light of the suns of the heavens around you and your neighbouring suns – the sacred suns of the near galaxies.

Even imagining, visualising, light qualities coming through you is hugely beneficial and effective.

Right now planet Earth is enjoying light from many, many sources that are newly directing their energies on her. This is raising vibrations world-wide, but the changes can cause confusion and also disenchantment with the status quo, which is what causes disruption in so many places across the globe. People are being awakened and they recognise what is not good, and seek to change it, destroy it. It is a time of huge upheaval. All will be well over time.

The light is throwing into full view those things which have been concealed and which must change; the corrupt governments and people with the wrong priorities whose actions are contributing to planetary problems. All will be revealed and visible and will be brought down and otherwise forced to change. Wrong action, inaction, will no longer be tolerated.

The righteous are strong and will insist on changes. The forces of light and galactic brethren are with you and will ensure the required changes are actioned. The light is shining through ever stronger and will only increase now. There is no retreat and no going back on the events now in process.

The love of light

Why do we enjoy being in the light so much? Different qualities of light offer different things to the perceiver; different possibilities. Light is complex. The bright clear light that is perceived after a cloudburst and then sunshine on a hot summer day is very different to the light that filters through warm sunshine late in the daylight in mid winter.

Light feeds so much on this planet. It is the source of and key to all. Light is everything.

And the quality of light on a gloomy grey day?

The light is still there, of course, albeit the intensity is obscured by the clouds. A bit like life for many of you. Light is obscured but it is still there. You need to part the clouds, eliminate or ignore them, and imagine the brilliant light shining through. A little trite but so true!

Commanders of the Light

These are beings across the universe who organise where and when new sources of light are to be directed to any planet or constellation. They work on the seventh dimension and also on the thirteenth dimension, and above. They are engineers of the highest order and use planetary and sacred geometry to orchestrate alignments, taking advantage of the respective aspects of the great cosmic patterns to bring about events and to ensure that the opportunities offered by the cosmic alignments are utilised to the greatest benefit and potential. They spot opportunities and often work and plan thousands of years ahead of what we perceive as time in their great work.

So the time of fruition of planet Earth has been foreseen for millennia and this forethought has enabled us to be here, ready and prepared, to participate in the evolution of planet Earth and the unfolding of the wondrous plan here. It is beautiful and it is perfect.

We have been practising life here in the third dimension for so many incarnations. Now is the life when it all falls into place and we take action to bring about the great change. Planet Earth; third dimensional to fifth dimensional. It will be done.

The Strength of Purpose

Our purpose defines us in so many ways. It provides a framework for our actions and the way we utilise and approach our free time (our time) and the opportunities we subconsciously offer to those around us and the universe to pull information to us to enrich and enlarge our lives. It is a statement to the world and those around us of what we value in life, indeed our values, and what we hold dear.

A being without a purpose is like a ship at sea without a rudder – at risk of being washed upon a shore without any bearing of where they are and what they can do there.

For many people their main purpose is to support and look after their family members and friends as a first priority. The day job is a means to earn money to fulfil the purpose of care of family and dependants. For others their main purpose is the role they choose in society – caring for people or taking active roles in the community. One singular purpose now could be to look after and prioritise the planet. If we do not do this we risk losing her, or at least losing the facility for life to exist and thrive on this planet.

All have come to planet Earth with a purpose and it is time for these to be revealed and acknowledged now so that we are all united in a common goal – to restore planet Earth to a sustainable, thriving planet which supports life in a healthy and symbiotic way so that all species may thrive, and which gives mankind a place to evolve.

Ask within to understand your purpose, your higher purpose, on the planet at this time. We have so much information within us. Our higher selves, our souls, know why we are here and what we have come to do. Our hearts guide us towards what gives us joy. Fulfilling our purpose should give us joy.

Purpose helps us to marshall our energies and to get things completed – which fuels and energises the ongoing purpose. When things we wish to accomplish are not achieved that can often create frustration and irritation. Right now, many people on Earth are having purposes thwarted. If your purpose is not what you want in your heart it may not be achieved. People who come from the heart and a clear understanding of their role and the end aim are more energised and single minded and more likely to achieve the goal.

*Where purpose aligns with the good of the self, the planet and those people around you then that purpose is empowered and is more likely to succeed. Right now, our planetary purposes **must** succeed. A sense of purpose gives us strength, and a clear goal keeps our energies aligned. These are powerful things. A purpose and a goal. The goal can change sometimes but if we are clear on what we are aiming to achieve then a re-think or re-alignment on the way is not necessarily a bad thing, (a review in how to achieve the goal).*

All mankind has a purpose on this planet at this time. Ask that your purpose be revealed to you.

The spread of the Word of God is something once only mentioned, it seems, in religious texts, propagated by scholars of the various creeds and churches. Now, more than ever, the word of God must go out in this modern age, this age of impending difficulties and tribulations. The word of God is to act to save the planet now. Stop the misuse of Earth's resources and take action to find new ways of living and being which respect planet Earth and the living entity that she is. The signs could not be any clearer that change needs to happen now, not in ten, twenty, thirty or fifty years' time. You don't have that long to wait.

Some of you are being given information about new technologies and steps that can, indeed must, be taken now to bring about change so that mankind's way of life is not so destructive to the planet and environment. For some beings on Earth her resources are so scarce where they live that they feel they have no choice about what they eat, or burn as fuel, and the consequences for the planet. In many respects this has come about because of the imbalances in food distribution or access to resources needed to develop communities that can thrive. Otherwise, where we live in relatively affluent communities and have a choice in how we live, we have therefore a huge responsibility to consider the impact of our choices on others and the planet and to respect and consider the options available to us and make wise, sometimes brave, choices. There is only one planet Earth.

The disruption brought about by the Covid pandemic on Earth is no accident. Ways of life have to change dramatically and this change has started as the world has responded to the impact of the disease. Many of these changes need to remain for the ongoing good of planet Earth and her environment and the varied life it supports. Mankind needs to use the effects of the pandemic, the changes it has brought, as a foundation for better decisions and better ways of living going forward.

Already communities are growing stronger, and developing, where little community spirit existed before. People across the globe are realising, or being reminded of, the joy that helping one another brings; the sense of wellbeing and knowing that there are people to hand who they can turn to for help. All communities should be more like that, relying on neighbours and the people close by to provide the necessities for living. A community resourced by and benefiting those who live within it. Thus a sense of identity and belonging grows for younger ones when they know and understand their origin, are appreciated for the contribution they make to the community, and have ongoing purpose.

Very wise individuals are being born on planet Earth now and they will not tolerate the rubbish and hypocrisy, the blindness and refusal to acknowledge what is happening on planet Earth. They will force through change at a cost relative to the resistance that societies put in as their refusal to find, accept and embrace new ways of living and being.

All are blessed.

Light intensity is growing on planet Earth. *As the intensity and quality of the light increases and refines, so more and more the darkness of planet Earth is lessened, and more is exposed* [comes to light].

Right now you are seeing the discovery of so much that has been hidden from view. The light exposes truth and cleanses, although different qualities of light, eg violet ray, can help in this process. So much is 'coming to light' for observance, acknowledgment and cleansing; the deeds, indeed misdeeds, of mankind; those events which have been covered over, covered up and hidden from view and public knowledge lest they inflame people's anger and bring shame to the perpetrators. So much that has been hidden and kept hidden will be revealed, exposed to the light, that reparation may be made, forgiveness expressed, as is appropriate. Forgiveness allows us all to move forwards. Not always easy.

Analogous to all this, the increasing light levels are cutting through the density of our atmosphere and the qualities of light are beginning to have an effect on organisations and materials; compounds, which could be described as pollutants. The light is exposing those compounds and as the light intensifies, as we move forward in the journey into the light, the qualities, nature and quantities of light coming in will enable and bring about changes in these compounds which will lead to their eradication, and thus eradication of pollutants. This is an aspect of light technology. The precise means to achieve this is being gifted to us, to dear ones on Earth at this time. But we can all focus on bringing through, bringing in, light and bathing planet Earth, and particular aspects of planet Earth, in the light so that light may perform its magic.

The violet ray is extremely good to use in this way; particularly useful. But other light technologies are coming through and it will be part of our collective responsibility to play our part as individuals helping to project and target this light, these lights, in the correct way in the appropriate places. It will be joyful work for all and we will see a difference before our eyes. Already we can bring in rain and quench fires, through collective action; this is just another aspect. Thought and light are the most powerful components of the universe and we will be using these tools to heal our environment – not to say ourselves too.

These are wonderful times ahead. Let all your actions be undertaken with love in your hearts and respect for fellow human beings and life on and of this planet.

All the colours within the light interact so beautifully. *These colours are all coming through to planet Earth as part of the rainbow light that is now so important. So much information wants, is required, to come through to planet Earth. You need it. Therefore the rainbow light bestows all that is required, perfectly. Breathe the light into yourselves and wear the stones that amplify that light. The quartz, the diamonds, the 'coated' stones. The rainbow cleanses and clears and bestows majesty on all.*

There are keys and codes embedded in the rainbow light that are helping mankind to move upwards now. Helping to enhance people's lives and their perceptions, uplift their moods and their outlooks. Clearing and paving the way forward for them. They need, however, to focus on this more. To move their awareness to consciously make choices that will propel them more quickly into the light and its offerings, rather than drift. There comes a point when people need to take charge of their destiny and to support those positive aspects that are taking them forward, so as to gain maximum benefit from the impetus.

Many areas of planet Earth are opening up now, literally like vortices into the earth. This is partly to enable the light to pierce any dark shellac and to move down into planet Earth. This action aims to access planet Earth's core, and her core beliefs and instinctive reactions, so as to be able to encourage her to limit her responses, potentially cataclysmic, to the great forces which are building up within and around her as a result of pollution and the desecration of the planet, or significant areas of it.

*Planet Earth **is** sacred of course but many areas have been devastated and Earth's natural response is like a wounded animal to lash out,* erupt in anger, and she is trying very hard, as a sentient being, to **not** react violently. We need to help her in this now. We all need to act in every way we can, as individuals and collectively, to remove, ameliorate, those triggers which are setting off planet Earth's natural, potentially harsh, response to the onslaught on herself and her resources.

So the vortices in the planet, and nexus points of force, can help with this as the light has clear passage into the interior, into Hollow Earth, to help alleviate the pressure within - with all the healing benefits of this beautiful light and the keys and codes it carries being beamed into and absorbed by planet Earth like soothing, healing balm.

We can all help by standing on the earth, outside preferably, with intent, pulling in the rainbow light from above us, from the heavens, and seeing it / visualising it coming down through us and into the earth from our feet, going down into the planet.

Imagine that light as a soothing ray; like soothing, cooling rain going down and being absorbed into the earth and inducing wellbeing. See it cooling raging fires of the underground volcanoes, clearing deposits of elemental treacle and tar; the treacle of negativity which also resides in our bodies as the result of negativity. Imagine the light vaporising this treacle into golden light to escape through the fissures of Earth and shoot upwards and outwards into Earth's atmosphere, contributing to a golden halo.

See planet Earth glow in golden light within and without; a reaction set off by the healing rays of the rainbow light both coming in and being absorbed and also being consciously channelled inwards by ourselves on the surface of planet Earth. It all helps. We can all help.

Turquoise – a splendid colour. *The ray of higher love. Turquoise uplifts, calms, soothes and comforts. Its recipients know they are held safe and secure and thus are peaceful. It is the colour of love when things are at an end maybe* [inference: end of life, although not exclusively] *and providing sustenance to those in that position.*

Turquoise evidently blends with blue and green and is a composite of their characteristics. It also motivates (its uplifting qualities) and enables a higher perspective, a higher view, and it is this which helps to elevate our consciousness. When we can see a bigger picture a lot more makes sense and this in itself brings understanding and peace, a deeper tranquillity.

Turquoise is the way forward. It is higher love and the key to our progression and ascension into the fifth dimension.

Higher love is what will take us through this now.

For every one of you who lives, resides, in the radiance there are ten, one hundred even, whose lives are in turmoil right now. It is the stage of things; the way on the path to change. All will come right. Right is not necessarily the joy of upliftment as perceived on this planet, this Earthly plane. Many of you came to planet Earth with a mission, your plan, to help elevate and clear away the negativity, and for some this means taking away, releasing, negativity as you depart this planet. In fact you will all do this to some extent regardless of your main focus, your immediate tasks. It is the case that for some this removal of a mass of negativity is your main purpose. You do it joyfully but the understanding may not be here until you have completed this mission, passing over as part of the process.

Ultimately everything is as it should be. It is progressing well enough, although many of you are stuck in worry about what is going on around you. Be mindful that your best approach is to disengage from the third dimension as much as you can and focus on the light ahead and those aspects of being that offer you, indeed bring you, joy and laughter and satisfaction. In clearing up the planet you are helping both the third dimension and fifth dimension, but if your focus is on the light and the purity you bring then the fifth dimension is amplified.

Try to keep your thoughts on the light and radiance you are helping to create / restore rather than focus on that which is not yet completed. That is to say, focus always on the positives, on the joy and help and support you can offer and bring rather than on what is not yet done. Does that make sense?

Those wishing to work with the fifth dimension. *First make the commitment that you wish to move into the fifth dimension. Embrace that ideal, that* **intention.** *Intention is all, as you know.*

'Remove yourself' from the third dimension as much as possible: news, conspiracy theories, people who talk constantly about news, pandemic – aspects of this time which relate to what was 'normal', ie getting back to how things were. That is your clue. There is no returning to 'how things were'. All need to move forward into a new future and create how things are to be; in many ways need to be, particularly for the planet.

Cut pollution in every way, change diet, change habits and how you live. Change plans in so many ways, eg travel. Aspirations need to change too. But there is so much joy and wonder our way.

We need to share the planet with all life forms and ensure it is habitable. More than that - a beautiful sacred and safe home for all beings. We need to give back to planet Earth now and stop just 'taking' and exploiting her for literally what we can 'get out of her'. This exploitation has to stop. We must go about our lives in a way which creates no harm; does no harm. We need to be creative about how we live, and we all need to work together.

Look at your life and examine it. Decide what changes you can make now to play your part in limiting the damage. Make that commitment. Do what are the easy bits for you and then think beyond to what else you can do. As more of you move towards this new way of being, of thinking, the easier it will become for others to join and come along too.

All actions undertaken must show respect for the planet. If it doesn't respect the planet ask yourself how you can do things differently;

what changes can you make to enable you to do things differently, even if not immediately.

The Purpose of the Fathers of Wisdom

The Fathers of Wisdom control the download of knowledge to planet Earth generally. There are many beings now on planet Earth who are divine beings with multiple consciousness from across the universe, waking up to and putting out into human consciousness the knowledge they hold in respect to wider civilisations and this universe, the multiverse even. They heed the guidance they receive individually about what to make public and what to hold back. The Fathers of Wisdom are among those who define, decide, what is to be made available.

Humanity as a whole is waking up now to higher awareness and many of you are open to and embrace the wider concepts and understanding filtering through. It gives you joy to receive this greater knowledge and answer some of the lifelong questions – 'What am I doing here..?'

The Fathers of Wisdom insist that light is a precursor to wider knowledge being allowed to come through as the light helps the 'enlightenment' process to occur in a balanced and meaningful way. Our aim is not to 'blow someone's mind' but to open it up to receive new information that can be assimilated in such a way as to be helpful, and to lay the foundation for more to come through on top of that foundation and to expand the mind and prepare for even more wonderful and fantastic realisations.

Those beings who elected to incarnate on planet Earth at this time have divine, varied origins. They are guided to find and uncover the knowledge that is right for them to receive at any time (the right time!) as it helps to unlock information innate within them. And this means that they can better receive and understand what is being revealed –

ie right information for them at the right place and right time in the right 'format'. It is part of the wonderful process of this universe. It all works in divine order.

Keys and Codes

Keys and codes assist this processing. Keys and codes, like light cells or packets that are held within our pituitary and pineal glands and our transpersonal chakras, that are activated to open up and expand our ability to understand and accept new information, and to make sense of it and build upon it. All beings can do this.

Some beings of the animal and natural world are awakening now keys and codes which will lead them to depart this planet permanently, en masse, ie to become extinct, their work on planet Earth done, completed. Some of this is indeed designed to shock and to stun mankind into opening its eyes to the damage being done to planet Earth and to enforce action. This has been happening frustratingly slowly so that ever more dramatic and cataclysmic events are programmed to occur so that the dangers, the perils, can no longer be ignored.

Whilst many of those who work to keep mankind in the darkness of ignorance use their power to insist that it's all sham and part of a natural cycle, the billions of people now awakening to the truth will accept this misinformation and misguidance no longer. It is like multiple wounds opening up and letting out poison. Planet Earth needs to be healed. Mankind recognises what needs to be done and the detailed information to enable the remedies to be applied is available. The Fathers of Wisdom are enabling this.

As of July / August (2021) Planet Earth is receiving a massive download of light that will pull her forward towards the great change that must occur now. [Further major downloads of light have since occurred, and will continue to occur, as appropriate.] *Planet Earth is shaking off those things that no longer serve her – just as mankind is being asked, urged, to do likewise and move into a new, light, more conscious way of being.*

Planet Earth is ridding herself of toxicity, just as mankind is being urged to move into a higher, more enlightened way of being, and rising above fear, ignorance, pettiness and lack of love in all its forms.

Gaia has always been a beautiful, wonderful and loving host to mankind – and other types of being and civilisations before that – but mankind's failing to see and understand the implications of actions are resulting in an overload of toxicity and imbalance of the systems she needs to maintain in order to function. That is to say, we are slowly destroying the ecosystems that enable planet Earth to maintain her fine and wonderful balance that allows life in its many and beautiful forms to exist, indeed co-exist, here. Mankind's way of life in this era does not allow for co-existence.

*Many incarnated, indeed most are here, to bring about the changes. Whether it is to help with the environment, invent and develop technologies that do no harm, utilising the new information being downloaded and made available to them via the Fathers of Wisdom, developing communities based on love and understanding that serve **all** life.*

Clearly we all need to consciously focus on love and respect for all life forms around us - fellow humans, animals, plant life, and in the air, seas and land water - to enable Earth to restore the symbiotic relationships which are required to allow and enable planet Earth / Gaia to thrive once more.

How to receive the downloads of information that will lead you further forward:

Bring in light daily as part of a regimen.

Consciously choose love and kindness as the basis of all your interaction with other beings.

Practice unconditional love (remind yourself that we are all wonderful beings and part of the Divine; we all have challenges and tribulations; most of us are 'doing our best'. Be kind, offer the 'benefit of the doubt'. Extend forgiveness; we are all imperfect and life is not easy for anyone, even if the difficulties and challenges faced may not be evident to us.

Resolve to be the best you can every day. Show gratitude for those good things in your life. Consciously look for and acknowledge those.

Look for ways in which you can help the planet, by changing / modifying your own behaviour. When you have done that, look for more ways to help the planet...

Look after yourself in terms of diet, exercise, and getting out into the natural world or finding a calm, peaceful setting. We can find peace in the middle of turbulence, with practise.

Receive healing from those connected to the universal light / Divine Source. Many are able to fulfil this service.

*Ask what you can do. Invite the light in to yourself and ask it to set the transformation process under way. If you are reading this the transformation process probably **is** under way but acknowledging and asking for developments may enhance and speed up the process. Be aware that change may not always be comfortable. Things that* *are familiar to you – habits, people even - may not be so central to your life as they once were.*

Life provides opportunities for growth and for us to be our true selves constantly, throughout the day. Once you start it becomes easier. Forgive yourself for any shortcomings and resolve to be your best at the next opportunity. Remember that you are part of the Divine. You have the capacity to be your divine self. It is why you came to planet Earth at this time.

The Two Suns

You were thinking earlier of the two suns that precurse the end of days. This phenomenon will occur only if the pollution around planet Earth is so excessive that a mirage effect is superimposed on the atmosphere as the strong light of the sun – with protections shed / stripped way – burns through the atmosphere and is refracted in such a way as to present a second, apparent, sun.

The light of seven suns is coming through now to planet Earth but these suns are not apparent. They lend their light to planet Earth's upliftment, with joy to do so. This strong cosmic light holds energies that Earth and her people need now to progress into the fifth dimension.

You have seen the darkness, the dust in the atmosphere above you as you view the land across the water. It is everywhere, unfortunately, even in your relatively clean island. The haze of dirt, fumes and dust rises and hangs suspended like a cloud. Unchallenged and unaddressed, it will blot out the sun as it has done in so many places now on planet Earth. You saw it even 30 years ago. Planet Earth is hiding her beauty as if behind a dark shroud of dense soot and smog. That veil of death must be cleansed and cleared.

You all must 'put your house in order' and then start to talk to Earth, to Gaia, the living, loving spirit of planet Earth. If she sees that you are taking strong action to remedy damage to her body and bringing in fundamental change she will listen. Act now.

The Move into Crystalline Beings

The human race, as you know it, is indeed done. Not in a negative way but a joyous progression into a form of life, a form of being, that has so much more capability to experience and participate in the many, many facets of this wonderful universe; truly moving into a wonderful new way of being as part of this divine creation of Source, the cosmos.

*You are to become fully cosmic beings here on planet Earth. Indeed you already **are**, you just don't yet see and understand it. But more are awakening all the time – to the illusion that has been cast on planet Earth for millennia and from the darkness which has enshrouded mankind and its awareness. Now is the time to wake up to the joy of being a part of the great divine creation. We are all masters. You on planet Earth are all masters. To each individual one of you, I say, 'Be it now'.*

How are we to become crystalline?

This will occur as a result of light quotient within our being and, again, once a few have undergone and completed this process it will become so much easier for others to accomplish this.

So light and DNA modifications will bring this about. Fifth dimensional beings will then be able to subsist on light and water for their sustenance. Other foodstuffs will be available (as I have told you) and the fuel for your light bodies is, no surprises here, light! And it will take mankind into dimensions and possibilities not yet explored within the compart of the third dimension. A move towards taking in more water, plants, and avoiding meat and dairy foods is an initial step towards the crystalline format. It will help to clear density and anything clogging up the internal machinery of man.

How are the DNA changes going to come about?

As a result of the light downloads and shifts, bringing consciously more light – which holds its own characteristics. Not just intaking of light but [through] keys and codes that are being triggered now. There will be special places on Earth that will assist this process.

Price of Love

There is no price of love. Love flows; love should flow. All things in the universe must flow for the patterns and plans, the great courses and routes of the stars and constellations across the heavens to complete and then recommence their great and grand journeys.

Part of the problem of planet Earth is that many things are no longer allowed to, able to, flow. Gaia and nature know best what she needs to maintain her beauty and stability, her ecosystem, to support the rich and magnificent life that once flourished on this Earth. Man's interventions, fiddling with nature and manipulation for greed, have disrupted the natural flow, the natural order of things. So now what? Gaia is in darkness and the life she supports is in distress or already gone.

It can still be fixed. Help is filtering through to the minds of the forces, the troops on Earth, the peaceful warriors. They have access to all the help in the multiverse. And implementing change becomes easier as mankind sees in ever greater clarity the disastrous impact on planet Earth and her communities of man's actions and activities - and more people awaken to the lies.

You are seeing now the effects of your actions on planet Earth. The evidence has been there for decades but in general you have chosen to ignore the warning signs. Now you can no longer do this. The writing is on the wall, as you say. Civilisations which have reached this point on other planets have been allowed to destroy themselves. This is not the path for planet Earth. You are surrounded by help; benign beings who will show you how to counteract chain reactions which have been set in motion. The gifts of information are coming through to light workers on this planet – indeed have been doing so for many years. The solutions are here but in many cases need more people behind them to create the mental force necessary to implement them and allow them to unfold.

In truth, mankind is not responsible for its inability to see and recognise the truth; its failure to take action. All that is changing now as people wake up to what is happening and who they are; the strength and beauty of their inner being, the recognition that there is a big job to do on planet Earth and that they have a duty to get involved and help to resolve this situation. All need to put their own house in order and not assume that 'someone else' will sort it out. All must do everything that they can now to save the beauty of Earth and the rich life that she has supported for so long.

I have shared before the power of thought. Right thought, focused correctly, will resolve and lead to the resolution of many of Earth's problems. You need to create in the right way to enable this wonderful work to unfold and be achieved. Only through unity is this going to be able to happen. All will be needed to unite to achieve the goals necessary now to help and restore planet Earth. All will therefore duly have a collective part to play and in unity inherit an Earth returned to pristine beauty.

Unity will save this planet. United in intent and united in thought, which has its own power which - used correctly - will resolve before your eyes issues and conditions you felt were immutable. You will see and understand so much. You will know and you will be successful. You are blessed.

Unity is key. It is the way forward in all respects. Unity of purpose, intention, thought and deed. You are all one, all part of the Divine. Does this not therefore make sense...how you would need to unite to solve planet Earth's problems?

Your disharmony is destroying nature, communities, the very fabric of planet Earth. Once you understand that and work together to restore balance and harmony things will change. And we will help you to identify and to carry through the steps required to achieve this.

It is all so simple when you can but see it. It all makes sense.

Many of you were Essenes and have spent lifetimes learning and living by the principles they advocated, before the time of Christ.

The Essenes, [who called themselves the Sons of Light], *were forerunners to this era, and that culture, sect, community, gave the environment and structure in which people could learn necessary rigours and discipline to prepare them for* **this** *epoch, this era. It was a vital part of the learning, the preparation. Many of you will have been part of the Essene community at some point. That in itself ran for 2,000 years. It had a distinct and wonderful purpose.*

The Essenes were forerunners to Christianity and set high standards and pure standards for life on Earth based on love, wisdom, understanding of a wider circle of beings, and the perpetuity of life. They lived in order, by order, but not under fear. Christ was an Essene [in incarnation in that era] *and many of you incarnated into that society to learn in preparation for this one. Many of you will resonate with the Essenes; the Essenes will resonate with people. It will provide a substantive link to which they can tether to help navigate what is ahead. That is why the Essenes are important.*

Look at the premises, the structure, the laws; they will carry through to form the foundation / basis of some of the fifth dimensional era. It is why the scrolls [the 'Dead Sea' Scrolls, apparently created by the Essenes and describing their community and values] *were able to be recovered and made public within the last eighty years or so. That society has relevance to today beyond a historical curiosity. It has meaning and purpose and people would be wise to familiarise themselves with this knowledge and the spirit / essence of that culture. Clearly some aspects are outdated and will not persist in the new age but much is very relevant still and a good indication of what is to come. Mankind's perception and abilities on a psychic front will be very much enhanced, however.*

There will be guidelines in the new way of being but all will be done in love and unity of purpose. Kindness too. No hierarchy; the new world order is one of love, compassion, understanding, unity of purpose and wisdom. A recognition that all are sovereign beings of mastery, awareness and higher purpose. We are a team of light on planet Earth, and in the heavens – the light collective.

[The Essene community was settled in Qumran, a desert site adjacent to the Dead Sea. Its inhabitants deliberately exiled themselves from the nearby city of Jerusalem in order to follow a more spiritual and ascetic life. The community adhered to a lifestyle involving rules or 'virtues'. The virtues of the Essenes were predated by: *The Law of One, a set of precepts that came to the fore in Atlantean times that developed as guidance on how to live in that Golden Age.* Possibly the virtues were based to some extent on these spiritual precepts. Living by a code, voluntarily; unity, community, love and respect. Living in the fifth dimension will be something slightly different – a 'higher' aspiration than the Atlantean Golden Age even.]

The Burden of Truth

What is the burden of truth? The burden of truth is the basis on which wise decisions are made, and must be made, for the greater good of all. Mankind is now faced with a burden of truth in that it can no longer dispute the environmental damage its ways have inflicted on Gaia and her natural systems, her ecosystems, and all life on this planet. The enormity of the situation cannot be ignored.

Steps must therefore be taken quickly, decisively, to rectify and remedy all sources of despoilment of the fabric of this planet. Gaia's very soul itself is damaged now, her hurt and disappointment coming through as a wave of destruction with the release of natural forces that she herself can no longer contain and suppress. Mankind's communities must change now if the planet is to survive. Beings on planet Earth can help both by changing the way they live, how and what they consume - no matter what society they live in – and by collective thought in a disciplined way which will release some of the psychological problems of planet Earth, because she is a living energy, a living entity, and she knows and understands when those beings on her surface are respectful of her or not.

If we can convey to Gaia that we wish to change, that we are doing our best and taking steps to change, she will redouble her efforts to help us to help her. To give us more time and space in which to produce coherent solutions to the many problems. But fundamentally mankind needs to work collectively, in unity and harmony, to resolve its issues. Our infighting is destroying not just ourselves – exhibited by wars and conflicts over the millennia – but now the very ground that our civilisation (if you can call it that; some light beings consider that term very funny!) is built upon. We need to stop the infighting and act now for the good of all, before 'all' is lost.

*There are people, light workers, who know how to approach and converse with Gaia and can explain. But she will be aware of the level of respect generally. We all need to respect, and show more respect – to work **with** Gaia now, urgently, and display through our actions that mankind **is** changing.*

The fifth dimensional planet is a visual construct based on the premise that what you envisage and focus on, you create. It is a representation of that power of manifestation. In your hearts and minds you create the 'heaven on Earth' so to speak: the beautiful, restored Gaia, planet Earth; thriving and lush natural life, and communities built on love, caring, friendship, respect, shared responsibility, sharing of resources. No-one is ignored. All built on love, light. All else flows from this.

We need to still sort out the third dimensional aspects, but the more we focus on this perfected idyll, the more within our grasp it becomes.

Talk to Gaia.

Lessons of Love

Love is what unites us. Gives us joy. It is the foundation of purpose since it is the love, the desire to enable or assist, to provide for, that underpins our actions. When we enfold someone in love we offer them protection.

We are programmed to love but we do have control over how and when to express love. When people hate they are suppressing that expression of their innate need to show love, and the inner conflict intensifies the feelings of hatred and destructiveness that exhibit as a result. Sometimes love is not expressed because of fear of self vulnerability or of becoming 'soft' or being unable to carry out tasks with objectivity. This is wrong since all actions should and need to be undertaken in a sense of love, with love underpinning all. True love is never wrong. And we should love unconditionally, allowing ourselves to express and feel love as the root and foundation of all actions. Respect is a fore-runner to love and indeed an aspect which begets love.

Love is infectious. It calms and settles, soothes situations, helps us to find the positives in every one and in all things. It is a gift – a gift to ourselves and a gift to all others around us.

When we gift ourselves with the ability, and give ourselves permission, to feel and express love that feeling of love multiplies and spreads to all aspects of our life. It has no boundaries. It changes our world, and it changes the world for everyone. Through love we can change the planet, and heal the planet.

These are times of tribulation *as mankind steps into hitherto unknown territory. Nature's forces unleash without control, it seems. All is not lost. We know what we need to do. We need just the courage and the wherewithal to do it. To apply the laws of balance and harmony that we know exist and that we recognise. To make manifest that which we know to be the correct paths.*

To a large extent the technology is available. We know, we recognise, what is required. We just need to apply it. Now. To have the courage to not hold back. To manifest the will of those who have stopped to think, or who have awoken to the perils we face imminently. Those who are here to take action.

Harvesting the Crops

So-called modern farming methods allow food crops to be sown and propagated almost around the year. The cycle of growth, the seasons, have been blurred to a large extent. The autumn harvest was a traditional time to give thanks for the crops, for the food to see everyone through to the spring and to the new source, new supply, from mother nature. To show gratitude for the bounty.

It is not necessary only to grow food perennially but it seems that mankind has forgotten to say 'thank you' to the Earth for what it gives, its rich bounty... Being so removed now from the source of our food, many barely acknowledge now whence it comes. Many children do not even understand that their food grows in the ground or grazes in fields or on land. Mankind must learn again to recognise planet Earth as the source of what keeps it alive and sustains it; to say, 'thank you', and show gratitude for all the crops and food.

Part of the gratitude is maintaining the earth in good condition, in respecting the earth and soil, the rivers and water systems that enable natural life and the crops and vegetation she supports and enables. [In] allowing the land to rest as required between growing seasons to help to restore nutrients to the soil, and to manage the land with appreciation, respect and gratitude; wisely, rather than pillage and plunder it like robbers and thieves intent on destroying that which sustains the life that planet Earth is trying so hard to support. Mankind's ignorance and thoughtlessness is killing itself.

Sadness

*Where does sadness arise from? Sadness arises from a sense of loss.
Loss of an opportunity, loss of a person, loss of a joy or benefit that
we felt we had, or could have had; had anticipated – and yet it has
not transpired or has been removed or withheld from us. Sometimes
our shortcomings lead to loss and sadness, and sometimes it is others'
shortcomings or actions, or the progression of life, as people move on,
and pass on.*

*Therefore take joy in the moments that you have that engender and
create that joy, that the joy may sustain you through sad times when
they arise, because this is likely to happen at some point, or threaten
to. Remembering joyful times can ease the pain and ache of sadness.*

*Earth is sad now, and many people on Earth at this time are
experiencing sadness of loss. Let not therefore the opportunities
that remain for redress and recovery, where ever they may arise, slip
away. Talk to and interact with your friends, family, neighbours and
those you come into contact with daily.*

*Welcome opportunities to show love, respect, honour – and fair
process – as they arise and are opened to you. Accept them and make
use of them to spread more love and respect. Spread positivity and
light within yourself and those around you.*

*Explain your gratitude to Mother Earth for everything that she offers
you, and continue your conversation with her to demonstrate that
you wish to help her, help planet Earth, and that you are changing
your behaviour and looking for new ways to do more. Let planet Earth
know that you honour and respect her, that you understand that as a
living sentient being she is experiencing despair, anger, sadness, and*

sense of being abandoned, and is demonstrating this through natural events, natural disasters which are her way of releasing built-up tensions, energy and imbalance.

Mother Earth is struggling to maintain harmony. She is a sentient being and if you talk to and communicate with her you can help her towards calm and enable her to moderate the outward sign of her own sadness and frustration. In the meantime act quickly to cull the damaging - and all - actions which disrespect Mother Earth. That is the only way now.

Havoc on Planet Earth

There is havoc on planet Earth as she strains and struggles under the immense pressure mankind has forced upon her. This is part of the wake-up call. Eventually even mankind cannot ignore the terrible cataclysm unleashing now on Earth - the fires, the tsunamis, the floods, the pestilence, the drought, the famine, destruction of ecosystems and nature, the pollution, the choked and toxic atmosphere, the death of huge sections of sentient life and the inability of the land to support life. Only when mankind's very existence is threatened will the truth sink in and people open their eyes and understand it is down to them to make the changes.

Havoc will continue and increase unless we act now to change the fundamental reasons for and causes of this condition. Planet Earth is like a wild horse, reined in, that can no longer bear the pain and frustration of restriction and is threshing and bucking wildly to break free; it cannot be pacified in any way. That is what we are asking of planet Earth.

The Theory of the Light

Light is cast on creation in all her aspects that we might see better; perceive better. Light enables perception and also reveals illusion. Light is clarity and power. Light is all that there is, but it is also a catalyst when it is brought into interaction with other aspects of its creation.

Light cleanses and clears the oceans. Light can destroy bacteria and organisms that are harmful or unhelpful. So light is a disinfectant. Light arouses the awakening of living, sentient beings, be it in the morning times so they know to go about their business in a new day, or as light deliberately and consciously introduced, re-introduced, into a being's energy system to herald and catalyse change, development and progression. Light quells darkness. When we bring light into our bodies and our energetic bodies we are bringing in — introducing - cleansing, clearing, purification and a transition into a higher way of being, because light automatically elevates.

The powers of light are mutable, influenced by the colour or hue of that light, which is a reflection of its vibration. These different colours are specialist; their attributes are specifics in bringing about certain tendencies and changes within and around the object that this coloured light is influencing.

Light beings, light workers, perceive that the light is a cleanser and tool for upliftment and awakening and ask it to bring this about, whether in connection with the planet, aspects of nature or sentient beings on planet Earth at this time. They may do this even without being particularly aware or conscious of their actions. Once light has cleansed and cleared, indeed purified, a being or object that being then has the space, the capacity, to take in more light and so the process of upliftment and progression towards the Divine is triggered and unfolds. It is a beautiful process which creates joy on its pathway. Sentient beings love light and are programmed to seek it out, seeking out darkness when they wish to be hidden from a predator or when they wish to sleep, ie retreat from wakefulness to rest, as light triggers activity in sentient beings.

Light will become a very important tool in helping planet Earth to cleanse, clear and purify herself. We will help her to do this – as beings of higher light and you on planet Earth (also beings of higher light, most of you, although only relatively few of you appreciate and understand this at this time; this will change very soon, and all will wake up to their responsibility to use the light creatively and for the good of themselves and the planet).

The Path to the Light

Some people choose to deviate on their path to the light. In some cases this is because of past life influences and for a need to experience certain situations. This might be karmic in origin — ie they have acted previously in a way which, universal law decrees, they have a karmic debt — that is, a commitment to experience, undergo, being in a set of circumstances which they may find difficult, awkward, uncomfortable, sometimes invoking responsibilities that may draw them aside from what might be the straight pathway into the light. It can incur a delay.

This is why some beings who incarnate on Earth in a condition of understanding and awareness are mindful that they wish to avoid creating karma of any sort — 'bad' or 'good' — as it can interfere with the progress to the light. Karma, however, no longer applies as much [as it once did] *on planet Earth as the planet and humankind progress towards a fifth dimensional shift, and new beings coming to this Earth tend to arrive free of karmic commitment and responsibilities.*

Once beings on planet Earth awaken to what they are — their divinity and their divine purpose — the quest for the light and to attain ever higher levels of understanding and perception is often unquenchable. It is a true yearning of the soul. As people awaken to the existence of their higher self — the being that holds all knowledge and awareness within and persists beyond individual lifetimes — they see the world through different eyes and this gift of knowing and understanding enables them to reach ever further into the light and find increasing joy along the way as their actions create a smoother path ahead.

That stated, not all spiritual growth is smooth. It can, indeed often does - because of the greater light that comes through - show to us, raise in front of us, issues and situations that may be tricky to handle initially. Loved ones who do not understand; parts of the being that may be in conflict.

All can and will be resolved but the process is not always comfortable or straightforward. The spiritual path is not an easy one yet cannot easily be ignored once one has committed oneself to the journey and set out on the pathway.

The Power of Love

This phrase has become a cliché in your world. It should be a statement that all sentient beings understand and apply consciously, for love, indeed, is all-powerful. It heals and resolves all situations in line with divine purpose and higher purpose. It sets all 'to right'. Love one another therefore and know that the love you extend is indeed a gift of higher purpose and initiation. There is no higher path than that of pure love, and extending light around the object of love, as part of that love. It is divine will in action.

Love has the power to transform at a cellular level. Love can heal all manner of ailments, bearing in mind that disease is exactly that – borne of dis-ease. Love helps an organism to heal itself and will indeed shortly be implemented more widely – worldwide indeed – in the healing of planet Earth. All humankind will have actual involvement in this wonderful process – to restore Mother Earth, Gaia, to balance and harmony.

As part of that love, mankind will show total respect towards planet Earth and in so doing will cease the damaging and deplorable actions that have created such mayhem. All facets of love will be employed in the unified effort to heal planet Earth and mankind.

As love on planet Earth grows manifold, the shift in consciousness that this promotes throughout sentient life, plus the doorways it opens to allow beings of light from other dimensions to make themselves known to mankind, will lead to even greater and wider types of tools becoming available for planetary healing and reparation - and that of other conditions that currently afflict mankind and are most difficult to assuage. It will be a wonderful and joyful time. All will rejoice. The birth of a new age. It is happening now and will arrive with exponential rapidity as mankind grows in awareness.

Masters at Arms

The light workers are now the Masters at Arms on planet Earth. Peacefully wresting away the power and authority of those who attempt to govern through fear and the perpetuation of falsehoods. Allowing the power and authority to be received into the hands of us all, unified in love, compassion, understanding and awareness of the great truth of planet Earth; what we are all, individually and collectively, here to undertake and to accomplish: the salvation of planet Earth and the move of all beings and planet into the fifth dimension.

There is no other way forward. Even those who perpetuate the lies and have invested their souls in the preservation of third dimensional living will wake up to what is true, in time. Their higher selves know the truth and always have done so.

The light workers are doing the work through bringing what is to the attention of all, helping people to wake up to what is happening on planet Earth in the third dimension and to the power they hold, the light they hold, as emissaries, part of the Divine. When people realise, bring awareness to what they are, the illusion of limitation falls away.

Truly, for all of us now, there is no limitation, and those who set out to convince and manipulate people into believing they are limited in power and capability, and try to retain power through fear, are promoting falsehoods and contravening the will and wishes of the universe. The perpetuators of falsehoods will too, however, eventually awaken to their own divinity. The fifth dimensional world is available to and welcomes all who wish to join in this new way of being, this love and light way of being.

The forces of light are all around us. *All around you. They cocoon mankind, even though you don't necessarily see, understand or appreciate that. They defend the divine order and the plan that unfolds now on planet Earth.*

You may feel dark times around you but in reality this is a time unsurpassed in great light, love, opportunity and new beginnings. It is the time of the rapture, so to speak, when all humanity rises up and is transported to a new era, a new way of being. None are excluded from this divine journey into immense joy and celebration. Even those who pass at this time - and feel the sense of relief and joy as they withdraw from this reality - relinquish their earthly bodies and understand; see clearly, for the first time for aeons.

All is well. All will be well – for mankind and planet Earth and the creatures that dwell on Earth; the life forms that she supports - many more than you can imagine, as life takes many forms that you may not yet understand. All is well. We are sending love. The plan unfolds as it is meant to. Mankind is awakening. Beings of light and love on Earth are moving forward, stepping forward, to take up the great cause for the light and moving into their spiritual roles here. The hierarchy of hatred, greed and sorrow is in decline. It cannot and will not persist. All is well. Rejoice therefore and redouble your efforts to grow into the light and take up your divine work, your divine role at this time. We love you all.

The source of light

Light comes from the mind of God, the will of the Divine. It is God's and God's only. It cannot be manipulated or meddled with. It is a manifestation of divine thought and divine will. It is of the most holy. Seek not to understand the source of light at this time. You know that the power of thought is all that there is. Consciousness, sentience, awareness, will, intention. Right intention. It is as simple as that. Blessed be all that understand and work with the light.

Mankind is in a third dimensional matrix and it is time to break free – to unplug. *You do this by focusing on the light, on the love and joy that connections and comradeship with your fellows and community provides. As you absorb light and extend it to others you will rise above the influences of third dimensional living and its restrictions and boundaries; its underlying precepts which are fear and control. This is now all falling away. The inpouring of light that pervades planet Earth is increasing rapidly, coming through to you individually via your stellar gateway chakra – one to two metres above the top of your head. This chakra then filters the light down through your energetic body first through other transpersonal chakras above your head and then into those connecting with your bodily systems, most immediately with your endocrine system.*

This influx of divine light is preparing you for your journey to the fifth dimension, which represents a higher way of living, of being, on planet Earth. All mankind is destined to move through to this new dimension which frees us from the shackles of a limited third dimensional existence and offers to all mankind opportunities, love, beauty, expansion beyond anything that can be imagined by most at this time. Mankind is on the cusp of realising its destiny as a fully aware community of divine beings. It is a time for joy and celebration. The more that you focus on the light and the possibilities, the realities that it is bringing through, the more quickly all beings on planet Earth will break through to that reality and move away from restrictions and density of the third dimension.

When we develop and embrace the love, the light, that is all around us we will automatically and very quickly change the way that things are done. It will no longer be difficult to implement the necessary changes. Obstacles which are currently appearing everywhere will fall away, just melt away, because all will be unified in purpose. You will be speaking to planet Earth en masse. You will be unified with planet Earth and working as a united force. Change can happen quickly, particularly with the help of outward (ie external to Earth) benign forces which are all around you to help if you could but see. All will be well.

So move upwards, move onwards, consciously bringing light into your bodies and working to eliminate and transmute the blocks, the dense emotions, worries and concerns that cloud the light within you. You can use the violet flame to help you do this. Call on St Germain and his helpers to assist with this. The violet flame can help you and help planet Earth at this time.

Many of you are actively communicating with planet Earth now. Many more will do so - as we recognise planet Earth, Gaia, as a living sentient being that is safeguarding, nurturing, and has been welcoming mankind to her 'being' / surface for millennia - and have the wonderful realisation that mankind and Gaia work as a team, along with all the sentient, non-human life that she supports. Mankind's eyes will be opened to a new band of compatriots on Earth that it scarcely realised were there – 'just' myths, legends; the echoes of a time when beings of all nature were recognised and accepted as companion bodies on this planet.

The renewal of light intensity will reveal all; enable mankind to see again. What we call the third eye, situated on the brow just above and between the eyes, enables this. It has been closed but is now opening for all. Mankind can work to consciously speed up and enhance this clearing and opening process – as part of the general clearing process of the physical and energetic body.

Gaia herself is now moving into a fifth dimensional space and as part of this process some features of the planet are disappearing. Some of the animals and plant kingdom are disappearing, going back to their home planets as they become extinct on planet Earth. Some of this extinction process is natural and some is a characteristic of the extreme situation on planet Earth whereby her ability to support life in all its variety is being hindered and hampered.

The extreme events on Earth in terms of environment and ecosystems are prompting some of the 'wake-up' that is happening now. As individuals become frustrated with the lack of will and intention on the part of governments to act, they are taking action and responsibility into their own hands, distancing themselves from the core of the third dimensional camp. As they move away they are able to see more of what is true. Their journey to the light gathers pace and is exponential.

It is a time of joy and celebration as mankind detaches from the matrix of confusion, masquerade and deceit and moves into the light and awareness.

The Light and the Love

Light and love are all around you if you but stop to be still and sense it. To a very large extent you perceive what you expect to find. Therefore be aware that the energy that surrounds planet Earth is saturated with love, highest intent for good, and nurturing, comfort and salvation of all. It is there as part of God's divine will and assisted by beings of light and love, the angels of the highest collective.

Be content therefore that you are looked after at all times. That all is taken care of, even if it sometimes may seem otherwise. Call to the beings of light to be with you and to assist you in all that you do. They are there and will respond directly to your requests for help in every situation. No person, man or woman, on Earth is alone now. The heavens are saturated with beings of love, light and purity from across the universe, the multiverse.

The more light and love you project to others the more will come back to you. It is part of universal law. What you put out you receive. Be aware of the light and love around you and it will magnify, multiply manifold. Consciously extend love and light as far and as wide as you can. Direct not only to those you know you love but to friends, acquaintances, colleagues, all with whom you come into contact, even to people you dislike and who you feel dislike you. The energy will change subtly, and all are worthy of and deserve love. Send it to all the animals, insects. Send love to all situations. It will transmute difficulties and uplift the energy; transform beautifully.

Send love to mother nature, to Gaia, your planet Earth. Together we are creating a new world order, the fifth dimensional order, that takes us all – planet and her peoples – into a beautiful, magnificent and wonderful new way of being.

Sovereign Beings

In mankind's progression to the fifth dimensional space it is important for each individual to establish their sovereignty. To insist on the respect of those around them that they are a being of strength and autonomy in that they have their own role and route / pathway towards the light of being that is therein and theirs alone to decide. No-one must dictate to them their pathway in life. This is an aspect of self-respect too. Each individual laying out, claiming their authority and right to self-determination. This need not be done without kindness and /or love. It may be difficult for some in some circumstances, however. When a being claims and owns who they are and tells the world: 'This is Me! I AM', let no-one say otherwise or attempt to subvert. Each has their own pathway that is theirs alone. Let no other being tell you that you are not you. Being yourself should not, however, violate the self-determination of others. Respect for all, all beings, is a tenet of our new age to come, that is indeed coming very quickly now.

The Gospels of Christ attempted to lay out principles and ground rules to establish a good basis for life on Earth but the times were different then, and mankind was still practising / honing its abilities on this third dimensional planet. Much information was subverted by ruling entities for their own purposes – again, a feature of the third dimensional matrix and deceit. It is all done.

We heal ourselves

Reconnect your being to the universe; awaken to who you are. Clear the blocks and blockages that limit and distort your existence on planet Earth, the conflicts of family and friendships that can sometimes tie us in knots and restrict us being who we really are. Take all actions *with love. That is so important now. Love must underpin all actions. Forgiveness is essential too. Disconnect from the matrix of fear, and do so by bringing in love to underpin your every action and thought. Love and respect, and forgiveness where appropriate or needed for all your fellow beings. It is the only way now. It is **the** way now.*

Bring in the light and let it do its work.

The light quotient

*Everyone has a light quotient - that is, a proportion, a representation of the light that the entity holds at that time. The light quotient for all beings on planet Earth and for Earth herself is increasing rapidly as part of the progress to the fifth dimension. Indeed this must happen for the move into the fifth dimension, to allow and enable the necessary changes to unfold. The light is a catalyst for more light. It is **all** light.*

On this day, [August 8] the Lion's Gate as some call it on planet Earth, the light streaming in to Earth and her inhabitants is unsurpassed. It is a very special day on planet Earth in light terms. It's like an influx of high capacity energy to jump start all – planet and people (and animals and elementals) into the next stage of work to transition to the fifth dimension. It will help enormously in awakening people who are still in third dimensional slumber and will shake up other things that need to be unsettled in order to bring about change. 'Disruptive technology' I think is the 'vogue' term of planet Earth at this time. Light is the ultimate disruptive technology. It underpins all technology since it underpins everything. You will know so much more about light in the coming days, months and years. It is all around you and yet most have no idea of its potentials.

*It really **is** all about the light, and beings from across the universe gathered to assist planet Earth in its growth process at this time* *are jumping up and down in their excitement to initiate and attune mankind into its many, many uses, some of which will be employed to assist planetary cleansing.*

There is so much enthusiasm, love and joy here. You cannot imagine how wonderful the events on Earth at this time are held to be across the universe. It is magnificent. You are all cognisant players in this too – most of you just don't see this at this time. It will change. Please trust us, dear ones. It is part of the planet Earth puzzle, the enigma, that we have found ourselves in. The solution is to hand, unfolding even as I speak these words.

The crystalline body - *our birthright on third dimensional planet Earth as we progress into the fifth dimension. All who physically enter / gain entry to the fifth dimensional space - the liberation of the fifth dimension - will have a crystalline body. They will be drinking copious amounts of water and suffusing themselves with light. They will be beacons of love, kindness, generosity of spirit – and most importantly they will hold and affirm to the belief that we are all equal in the eyes of the Divine; that we are a unity of purpose, love, responsibility and sacred intent. There will be no happier intent than these of planet Earth at this time. The sacred ones. The door is open for all to be sacred ones. You are all here by right and invitation. The door is now wide open. Make your choices and choose well.*

*You can speak to your own body; inform it and prepare it for the changes that are to be made. Let it know that its biochemical structure will be changing, indeed **is** changing. Feed it with light, love and water; a wholesome light diet of nutrients, plant based. There are no 'do nots' but you can make the process easier by adopting a diet which is free of harmful substances that your body needs to work more intensely on clearing from you physically. Essentially you are giving your body less 'routine' work to do and allowing it to undergo changes in the time that is freed-up from otherwise battling ingestion of toxins. There will always be toxins and substances coming in, being ingested, that aren't so desirable, particularly with Earth's pollution as it is, but you can help your body to minimise or at least reduce the workload on that front.*

Healing your body, preparing your body, is no more complicated than high and right thought. You can talk to your body and explain to it what you wish it to do. You can talk to your subtle bodies and explain to them what you would like them to do. You can talk to your body elementals and ask or indeed tell them what you wish them to focus on and undertake. You have so many tools at your disposal.

Mankind should be aware that everything someone puts into and holds within their body has an effect. Not just food, liquids, alcohol, drugs etc but also the thoughts and feelings, the outlook and perceptions they hold; their whole demeanour. Thought lays the foundations for so much else; it is who we are, or who we appear to be. So back to the premise that we can change our bodies, eventually our structure, through thought.

The Wonders of Light

*I could speak all day about the wonders and capabilities of light. Light engenders more light to a point where that is all that is. We **are** light. The crystalline body will engender even more light and take mankind into realms and possibilities beyond your imaginations now. It is a wonderful future of light, love, opportunity and actuality. You will all converse with light beings as if it were nothing special, so different will your lives and your experiences be. There is no limitation to the joy that you will encounter and embody.*

Your light bodies, your crystalline bodies, will take you into realms of light and actuality beyond your comprehension. I state 'actuality' because it is a different state to 'reality'. Actuality is a state of being, a point of being at which there are no boundaries and at any point all is possible. You have unlimited possibilities at all times. That is actuality and many of you will be there before you even think you might be there. It is a state of possibility without boundary, governed only by your imagination – and your imaginations will be way more expansive at that stage. It is total freedom, unbounded. A totally pure state of being. You will become light. You are divine beings and you will become divine light. Such a wonderful prospect for mankind.

It is just beyond grasp at this time but will be within reach very soon. In a state of actuality anything is possible at any time. Total flux.

What is a Crystalline Body?

In a crystalline body the light intensity has reached a point where all fluidity is possible due to the light quotient. Sense contradicts this since you regard, understand, crystal as solid and the opposite of fluid. In fact, nothing is solid and you will be fluid beings, like shape shifters, and due to your light quotient will appear as crystal when you take on solidity.

The fifth dimension is a different realm, a different dimension, remember. You cannot compare what you have known with an environment that you do not know, do not understand the characteristics of beyond a few rudiments. There is much information available now about how joyful it will be, the unity and brotherhood and sisterhood of communal purpose, understanding and respect. But of the characteristics of what is possible there, in that dimension, there is relatively little. Trust, and move forward.

In fact there is a choice – you can choose to remain within a third dimensional environment along with the serial challenges and tribulations third dimensional planet Earth and her inhabitants have experienced for millennia. But why continue to suffer? Why continue with burdens, sorrow and manipulation by others when you are offered freedom, love, light and unlimited joy and truly wonderful possibility beyond anything you can imagine at this time?

Trust, resolve and take steps to move forward. Have courage.

The Quest for Being

When souls incarnate at origin, ie are created as spirits, there is a clean slate. They develop and grow as they are nurtured, in accordance with controlled conditions around them. They are like fledglings that are strengthened and succoured for flight.

At a point they are released to develop and find their own way in the universe, in the multiverse. They choose their experience, just as mankind on planet Earth has chosen its experiences – individual and collective.

You have periods across the aeons which are recognised as important, or spiritual, for various reasons in that they are landmarks in history, either because they are developmental milestones or fascinate in some way, eg the Egyptians, the Incas and great civilisations that have risen and fallen across the globe. Lessons learned. Transformations achieved. Sometimes grand failures.

All on planet Earth is now subject to, at risk of, falling. Yet this marks a pivotal change, a major shift, in the annals of mankind on Earth. It is perhaps the greatest story that will ever be told on planet Earth as she transitions to a fifth dimensional format, the fifth dimensional matrix.

Bring light into your heart therefore, take courage into your hands and step forward to take up your role in this metamorphic change of planet Earth and mankind. All here on Earth have a role, including you.

We can Talk to Planet Earth

We can talk to planet Earth. We can tell her that we appreciate her and understand the pressures we are putting on her. That we are doing our best to change the way we do things. Tell her that we love the nature she supports – the birds, animals, insects, sea creatures, plants and vegetation. That we understand that Earth is a complex ecosystem that mankind is in danger of totally destroying. That we have become dangerous.

Gaia naturally acts to destroy and remove those influences which threaten the fine balance and continuity of her ecosystem. Unfortunately mankind has become her adversary in this respect and she will act to destroy us if we continue on our present pathway.

Pagans were persecuted but actually did a huge service to all by acknowledging and honouring and giving thanks to Gaia; the seasons. Their actions fed the planet and ensured her connection with mankind was two-way, and a firm bond. Mankind listened to her. The orthodox Christians, in ignorance, tried to drive out this awareness and severed the links between man and Gaia, which is the support system for mankind's existence on planet Earth.

Paths have since diverged and mankind grows increasingly distanced and removed from awareness of planet Earth and her magnificence, and our reliance upon her. Mankind thinks technology is the saviour. We need to think again.

There will be guidelines on the new way of being *but all will be done in love, and unity of purpose. Kindness too. No hierarchy; the new world order is one of love, compassion, understanding, unity of purpose and wisdom. A recognition that all are sovereign beings of mastery, awareness and higher purpose. We are a team of light on planet Earth and in the heavens – the light collective.*

The extreme events on planet Earth – weather, natural events, fires, wars, famine, drought - are acting to pull sentient, aware mankind together and bring out the finest aspects of their beings, as the third dimensional world as it has been cast, organised, falls away; all that has been fairly solid and sound in terms of a set way of life – which allows and allowed mankind to ignore so many signs and impending difficulty and change – falls away. Certain areas that remain stable do so in order that a regimen can be initiated to underline the changes in approach to life and planet that are necessary now. Nothing can 'wait' any longer.

But you can all help, right now. By embracing light, love, caring and compassion for your fellows. Changing, bothering to change, the way that you do things. Talk to the planet and the environment around you. Acknowledge all forms of life – plants, animals, insects, elemental beings. Acknowledge that stones and shells may prefer to be in their natural environments, that crystals may wish to reside in the earth where they can perform their functions at this time. All have purpose on this planet. Be open to this and acknowledge it. Talk to these beings, even telepathically – telethought.

The Variations of Love

There are many forms of love; nuances. Essentially love is light in its form as an emotion. Love **is** light, an expression of light, and like light has nuances, characteristics that we define on planet Earth and identify by different 'words' – romantic love, loving kindness, love of friendship, love of parents for a child, for a relative or dear friend. Unconditional love, which is total regard and respect for all around us individually, respecting and honouring each one as a part of the Divine, and therefore as a part of ourselves.

Understanding this connection is a first step towards unconditional love. Love has no boundaries. It uplifts the one who loves and the one who is loved. It takes us into a dimension where we are our divine selves, a part of God. Choose to love, therefore, rather than hate or dislike. Where it is difficult to love another – one who is a feature of your life – then you can actively try to find aspects to love or like, to see the good in all others. Try the Ho'oponopono prayer as there may be energy between you that makes the reason for the conflict between you unclear. It will transmute the energy and clear the sense of dislike or inability to love. We all need to start doing this now. We all need to love and to practice and practise unconditional love.

The love of nature, of animals, of birds, plants; the natural world. Love and respect for Gaia who supports us on this planet and who is clearly distressed at this time.

Love also offers protections on an energetic level to those around us. Love puts a protective shield of light around someone that offers protection on an energetic level and can help to heal dis-ease in certain circumstances.

Light mends cells. Healers, when sending light, direct light energy. Love is another way to encompass someone in light, to direct light energy. It's a natural response. We need to make unconditional love - to hold and extend unconditional love - a natural response to all interaction with our fellow beings. To unconditionally love the being; not necessarily the being's actions, ie we separate the being, the divine aspect of God, from the action that we do not like or condone.

Intention is enough. So important. Set your intention to love all others unconditionally, to see and accept that they are all part of the Divine. That all mankind – and light beings; we are all part of the Divine. We are loving ourselves when we extend, exercise, unconditional love.

People need to awaken and they will find within themselves the divine self that exists beyond this life, this lifetime. The divine self that is their true self. This awakening will unlock and reveal to them the understanding of who and what they are, their origins and their role on planet Earth at this time. It will be a powerful awakening.

Many of those still asleep and not aware of their true selves have the capacity, the purpose, to unlock greater knowledge and pieces of information that are part of the final puzzle we are putting together on planet Earth.

The roles of mother and father have been eroded, been merged to some extent as the divine feminine energy has strengthened and become more powerful on planet Earth in very recent times. It is part of the balancing. The role of the father – masculine energy – is still important, of course, but the divine feminine energy is appearing paramount now as the pendulum swings in 'her' favour before perfect balance is achieved / realised.

The female presence in a household; the male presence, are different things slightly as the traditional male presence was one of provision, order and authority whilst the feminine energy / presence was one of nurture and care, the aim being that the two are complementary.

Single parent households and wider issues, change, have eroded the joint responsibility in many instances. So a strong mother figure now emerges to cover both roles and, similarly, a 'kinder', softer, masculine figure which embraces roles of both provider and carer has also come to the fore. All this for the sake of the children and those who rely on the nurture of a household and home as they grow and develop. It is mankind adapting to circumstances. It is also a wonderful learning situation for all concerned, and which some choose to be in to facilitate and enable this particular learning. They are blessed, as are all of you on planet Earth.

The heart is the core of your being. *It is your powerhouse, the internal engine that keeps you going and all in good shape. It is also the psychic centre of your being. Focus on the fifth dimension and not on the third dimension. There is too much focus on the third dimension at this time. Go to the fifth dimension more often.*

The forces of darkness are again collecting over Afghanistan. *They will be dispersed but not before Earth has undergone her final, and vital, challenges and tribulations. All will be well. Remember that.*

The soil under the feet of mankind will burn and there will be drought and sorrows worldwide. It will be cataclysmic. Hold fast dear ones. Bring in the light to yourselves and allow it to uplift you and burgeon you in your times of need. Help others and extend light as much as you are able to. It will reflect back to you, such is the nature of light. Have courage and hold joy in your hearts. It is the final scenario coming in to play now.

The Purity of Light

Light refreshes, uplifts, cleanses and clears, as you know. It is like a crystal-clear mountain stream cascading through you, washing away all traces of silt, sand, stuck energy and pattern of past trauma that can be lodged into being. It is a cascade of new being, new energy, new possibilities and opportunity running through the self and the body. Consciously taken into and through the body, it can cleanse and clear all 'stuck-ness' and stagnancy and wash away illness and dis-ease.

Light is the healer; the master healer. Its propensity to help grows as the understanding and openness to its power and capability grows. It can achieve anything if the conditions are suitable to enable this – lack of 'known requirement', a certain acceptance and openness to huge change at a fundamental level. An understanding and openness to the idea that light can cleanse, clear and heal all ailments. We open to universal possibility and the universe responds. What is only pure water, with pure light running through it, was used in baptism. A rebirth in the cleansing water. It is symbolic but it is more than that. A molecular change is brought about. Bathing in light can bring about a similar magnificent rebirth of possibility. Like a slate being wiped for the new information to be laid down.

The wonder of what is possible is limited only by our imaginations. Therefore let your thoughts be expansive and reach high - into the heavens and higher dimensions. Seek there and you will find God, the Divine and divine answers and solutions to your problems. It is so.

The Light of the Fifth Dimension

The light of the fifth dimension is growing now on planet Earth, acting as a glowing flame that attracts all beings of light throughout the universe. Most that need to be here at this stage have come; others will follow as the time is right.

To move into the fifth dimension set your intention for it to be so... Love, light, kindness. Stand your ground in what you know to be good but avoid unnecessary conflict. Maintain serenity as far as possible. Ground yourself daily. Bring in light consciously and direct it to those around you. It will help you to maintain a serene and calm environment. Think positive thoughts. Help the planet and yet know that what is happening is part of her path too. Understand and accept that. Talk to planet Earth.

As the energy of the planet and its surrounding aura shifts and absorbs increasing amounts of light your light quotient will increase - and you are already on the road, the path, to the fifth dimension. Your actions can speed up progress. We are all going there at some point. Ask what is your role at this time.

The light that is coming through to planet Earth now *is of unsurpassed magnificence of what has been seen hitherto. The light indeed carries keys and codes, resplendent in their potential, and actively to move forwards, shift, mankind at this time. Light is the fluid, the fuel for all transformation – the matrix carrier that absorbs all negativity and bursts forth in rainbow showers to cast light, love, purity and blessing on all beings. It is the illumination of God's perfection.*

Rejoice in the light; bathe in the light. Light's being is energising, and you need only to ask for the light to come into you, to bathe your physical and mental ills, and it is there for you. There is no end, no limit, to its capacities and healing propensity. Light is the medicine of the future, and of the now. Light is God's, the creator's, raw material. It is blessed. It is all that is.

Light is infinite. More facets will open up to mankind in due course. Bring light in to your bodies and feed on the energy, the strength, the purity and the purification and growth it offers. Light is the key to entering the fifth dimensional reality, the fifth dimensional world. It is coming in for all beings on planet Earth and for Gaia herself.

You can accelerate your own progress into the higher dimensions by consciously bringing in light into your body and energy systems and grounding it into planet Earth. Do this now, as often as you are able to, daily preferably. Let all move collectively into higher light and rejoice in the radiance.

Amen.

We will be shape shifters. *It will be an option to display crystalline facets. Most powerful healers will work as crystals to refract, absorb and reflect the greatest amounts of light. We do this to some extent anyway, working with the light, but this will become more pronounced.*

Principles of Existence

*Planet Earth has long been prepared to host mankind in its various forms. It was once a fiery planet and could go that way again over the long timescale. Things are of course very different now but care and attention are required to yet cultivate and maintain Earth's suitability to support life as you know it. You, mankind, are all here to facilitate the evolutionary process. You just don't 'know' it consciously, or most of you anyway. This **will** change over the coming decade or so.*

Many of you are waking to the wonderful reality, truth, of what is mankind – Adam Kadmon – and what is happening to the planet – indeed must happen to the planet if she is to survive: Ascension – transition into a fifth dimensional format from the third dimension which has persisted for so many thousands of years.

It is a progression into a reality where the rules / laws of physics which govern how this planet and all life on her work are changed, upgraded if you like, so that finer, in some ways more sophisticated, formats allowing greater fluidity and freedom of expression, of being, of communicating, of manifestation and getting things done and to happen, become the 'norm' rather than the rare exceptions which you hear about from time to time and are regarded most often as extraordinary.

*It's a progression to a new 'ordinary', a very wonderful ordinary. It will be amazing and joyful... Even those who are resisting the change will be 'won over' in time when they see, understand, and begin to appreciate the beautiful perfection of the new ways in which we can **be**. The peace, the love, the serenity and tranquillity. The release and dissolution of boundaries and limitation within which the third dimensional format has imprisoned mankind.*

The joy of all the heavens is with you on planet Earth now. *We rejoice as we see the Grand Plan coming together – all here are aware, however, that for you on Earth these are not comfortable times. It is the plan. Not to frighten, but the plan to cleanse and clear the aeons of negativity; to provide the clean slate of purity that must be in place for the new world to embody and develop.*

The excitement among the bodies of great light and illumination is that all is coming together beautifully. In fact you are doing more than well in toppling the masters of guise on planet Earth. Soon you will all understand the Great Plan and you will rejoice too. You are all so blessed.

The Symphonies of Light

Light has a sound. Light is a vibration and all vibrations create sound, and therefore light has a sound. A very high vibrational sound – the highest in the universe. This is an aspect of healing. Remember that all things are connected; all comes from the same Source. Light therefore is the master healer, and sound is a derivative of the light.

Different sonic vibrations create different effects. The right use of light, of sound, will enable mankind to resolve many of the problems facing planet Earth at this time. You will receive help from those of the many light beings surrounding Earth who are specialists in this field. Information will be downloaded to those whose role this is to undertake these healings, to apply this sacred method at this time.

The birds in their natural air habitat hear the sound of light of this elemental sphere more clearly than other species currently and are benefiting from this as the light downloads to planet Earth increase in amount and quality, diversity and vibrational essence. Other species will follow.

Some of your brethren are attuned to sending out sound; who have the capability to heal and alter the substance and nature of things through their voices. They do this intuitively and hone their abilities through raising their own vibration. Both deep and high tones are helpful in different circumstances and to address different things. They know what they do. They are mainly led by their subconscious and open to instruction and guidance from the light beings around them who support them in this special sacred work.

Some of them also speak and understand light languages, and their tonings are of course an aspect of this mode of communication. Light language may also be expressed as symbols which many now on planet Earth can perceive and understand the meaning of. These are part of the keys and codes that are being downloaded to us all in these days of increasing harmony and connection with the light. So you see that all is interconnected. These keys and codes are part of the universal language of light and love. We are all indeed all one. Everything is one. Every aspect of the universe, the multiverse, is one.

Together we can think this planet back to health and wellbeing through the right application of light, sound and love. We are all one.

That is why the vibration created by sounding 'Oohhmmmm...' in your being is helpful to you. It raises your vibratory rate to a higher level, creates a feeling of wellbeing, clarity and positivity. All manner of positive result.

If you can distract yourselves for even a brief period of time from the 'doing' all around you and stop, and pay attention to your self, you can achieve what some might consider miracles in transforming your life and the world that surrounds you. Even one person paying attention and changing their microcosm can make a difference.

Together we will change this world and this is exactly what we have come here to do. Our roles to undertake and complete.

The gates to the fifth dimension are now wide open. *All are welcome; all may enter. Think hard about your priorities now, what is important to you and to your families, your loved ones, as you negotiate these challenges here on planet Earth. We know as we look around that there is strife and difficulty, fear and sadness and unease.*

There is joy, celebration, acceptance and understanding beneath the façade of pain. There is joy in all things waiting to be uncovered, revealed. Move into a closer association with the Christ light. Draw it into yourself as you go about your day and you will notice the dispersal of heaviness. The light clears and cleanses all; healing all, in time. Reduces burdens.

We are all here for a purpose. Ask for the light of the universe to come into you. Ask for the light to reveal to you your divine purpose at this time, in this place, on beautiful planet Earth.

All challenges are opportunities for growth, and that is our eternal purpose. Growth, understanding, recognition of our own individual magnificence. We are all magnificent beings of love, light and purity.

Anything else is illusion.

Afterword

Archangel Metatron (11 October 2022)

Our understanding and ability to effectively use light will grow and expand as we grow and expand as a collective moving into the fifth dimensional space. It will be a space where thought defines our ways of life and how we experience planet Earth. Our collective power, and transition into a lighter way of being, will enable us to find and apply solutions to so many of the current issues facing planet Earth.

What we think, we create — now more than ever — and it is vital therefore that we discipline our thoughts towards positivity and love, committing to a way of living that allows all humanity to contribute to a joyful existence.

Much will change very quickly now. Some will descend into darkness but we all have the opportunity, the choice, to move forward into a peaceful experience of this world.

Much light will emanate from the centre, the core, of this planet and will inspire mankind into the recognition of unlimited possibilities and sense of joy, excitement and adventure into a new reality.

Appendices

Adam Kadmon: The light body / light manifestation of man, woman.

Axiatonal Lines: Energy lines that connect the electromagnetic circuitry of beings with corresponding / resonating circuits and systems in the cosmos.

Body Elementals: Sentient energies, representing the elements of earth, air, fire and water, present in the body and with responsibility to autonomously carry out functions pertaining to their element on behalf of the body to ensure good health and vitality.

Coated Stones: Crystals, frequently quartz or quartz family (eg amethyst, citrine), that are coated with a layer of a material such as gold, titanium, copper. Crystals treated in this way are often known as 'aura' and may combine the benefits of the crystal and metal. They often project a 'rainbow' effect.

Essenes: Ancient mystic Jewish sect, calling themselves the 'Sons of Light', self-exiled from Jerusalem and living in the wilderness of Qumran, close to the Dead Sea, in the two centuries before the birth of Christ. A collection of writings known as the Dead Sea Scrolls were discovered in 1947, and throughout following years, in caves adjacent to Qumran and were attributed to the Essenes, the scrolls' writings outlining their community and its strict spiritual and ascetic values and way of living in which they voluntarily adhered to a system of rules or 'virtues'.

The Fifth Dimension: a higher dimension, a higher vibrational space, than the third dimension which we currently experience on planet Earth (although we and the planet are already evolving). The fifth dimension is a reality that might be likened to the (fifth dimensional)

Garden of Eden ('Heaven'). It is a space where light illumines everything and where different rules of the universe apply, enabling a very different way of living, with possibilities and opportunities beyond what most of us can imagine at this time.

The Great Invocation: (given to us through Alice Bailey, author and Theosophist in 1937)
From the point of light within the mind of God
Let light stream forth into the minds of men
May light descend on Earth
From the point of love within the heart of God
Let love stream forth into the hearts of men
May Christ return to Earth
From the centre where the will of God is known
Let purpose guide the little wills of men
The purpose that the Masters know and serve
From the centre that we call the race of men
Let the plan of love and light work out
And may it seal the door where evil dwells
May light and love and power restore the Plan on Earth

The Plan on Earth is (understood to be) referred to by Archangel Metatron in these channellings variously as The Divine Plan for Planet Earth; the Grand Plan; The Great Plan; and is part of a Great Master Plan.

Grounding: A process that enables us to strengthen our connection with the earth by aligning our energy with Earth's energy, and which may enable us to better focus our mind, intentions and actions. There are various approaches to grounding: standing / walking barefoot outside on land or in water; by swimming; by visualising light coming from above into the top of our head, down through our body and out from the soles of our feet and flowing, like roots, deep and strong into the earth and around rock and crystal. The analogy is that of a tree with strong, deep roots, which give that tree strength, support and protection against elements which might otherwise damage and even uproot a weaker tree.

Higher Self: That part of us that knows we are part of the Divine and of God. That essence of our being that recognises who and what we truly are, why we are here, our purpose, the learning we need to take away from our time here when we embark upon our adventure on planet Earth. It knows what is 'right' for us at any given time; the path to take for our way forward to achieve what we set out to fulfil in the current lifetime. Quieting our mind, meditating, may enable us to connect with our higher self, which may show us the way to our passage through life, in issues great and minor.

Hollow Earth: Interior of planet Earth understood to host an advanced civilisation in touch with and engaged with the spirit of the planet, Gaia, and also with extra-terrestrial beings of light. Various access points including via the north and south poles and certain sacred sites and high dimensional locations.

Ho'oponopono Prayer: A prayer of forgiveness and self-healing originating in Hawaii, based on the premise that we frequently cannot know the source or origin of strife, dislike or distrust of another being as this may be related to a past (unrecalled) life. The prayer, stated repeatedly whilst focusing on the person / situation, can transmute negativity: *I am sorry, please forgive me, I love you, thank you.*

Karmic Debt: Accumulated energy from this and past lives; frequently negative and requiring 'good deeds' undertaken to 'balance' the karma.

The Law of One: All comes from the one Source and all relate to it. We are all part of the One. The actions, thoughts, of one element affect all elements. We therefore have a collective responsibility, and the law reminds us of our responsibility to self and to the collective whole. As part of the Law of One, certain principles and precepts – upheld - work to honour, safeguard and protect the sanctity of the individual and the whole. Principles such as grace, forgiveness, purity of thought and deed, unconditional love, recognition that our thoughts shape our future are examples in these writings. Metatron has stated the importance of the principles of the Law of One alongside the 'virtues' of the Essenes mentioned in these writings. There are other facets of the Law of One, strands of guidance, which will be revealed, become evident more widely, as we all move forward. All is revealed at the right time. Archangel Metatron has stated that the Law of One is as old as the cosmos.

Light Quotient: See Spiritual Light Quotient.

Metatron's Cube: Primordial form of sacred geometry believed in its complex (three-dimensional format) to hold all the geometric shapes on which all creation is based (the platonic solids). Its 13 spheres align with the 'Seed of Life', which in turn aligns with the 'Flower of Life', both further sacred geometrical shapes. Metatron's Cube represents balance and harmony. All three forms hold huge intrinsic power and mystical significance.

The Rays: The colour rays are ways in which light colour propensities are classified according to their attributes and capabilities. Originally seven rays, these are to be expanded. Master beings are assigned responsibility to the individual rays and govern their use and attributes, which may change in response to requirement.

The Seven Sacred Suns: These are suns mainly in constellations within this galaxy, the Milky Way, from whose constellations many of the 'light collective' beings currently assisting and safeguarding planet Earth are drawn.

Spiritual Light Quotient: All beings have a light quotient. That is, a proportion, a representation of the light that an entity holds at that time. It reflects that entity's capacity to understand spiritual concepts. The light quotient for all beings on planet Earth and for Earth herself is increasing rapidly as part of the progress to the fifth dimension.

Stellar Gateway: Energetic centre (chakra) of the human form. Positioned approximately one to two metres above the top of the head. Major access point for high frequency light to enter our being.

St Germain: Ascended spiritual master being regarded as having lived various high profile spiritually orientated lifetimes on planet Earth before his ascension into the light. Responsible for the seventh ray (violet) and bringing forth the violet flame for transmutation of negativity, and thereby a pivotal role in bringing humankind also towards transformation into the light.

Talk to Planet Earth: We can do this in meditation, by focusing our thoughts with love and positive intention on planet Earth, by following our intuition. Or by speaking aloud to the planet, or to elemental beings, to animals, to all sentient life. We are all connected. We are all One.

Telethought: Term given to Channel by Pleiadian beings referring to a process in which messages can be transmitted to other beings in general by focusing on / sometimes stating out loud, and visualising, the message content with the specific intention of it being distributed / relayed to a specific audience or place or in a specific direction / across or surrounding the planet.

Third Eye: Energetic centre (chakra) of the human form positioned in the centre of the forehead directly above the eyes. Associated with 'sixth' sense faculties such as intuition, higher awareness, perception; 'seeing' and being aware of what is not generally perceptible from a physical standpoint. The lesser spoken of fourth eye and fifth eye energy centres are positioned vertically above and aligned with the third eye on the forehead.

Violet Flame: An immensely powerful spiritual energy, emanating from the **violet (seventh ray)** with the ability to cleanse, clear, alchemise (transmute) and uplift. It can be applied to all sentient beings including ourselves, animal and plant life, to situations, to all aspects of the planet, and beyond. Overseen by St Germain, and widely understood to be a gift to humankind at this time of evolution.

The Void: The void is a state of nothingness, of emptiness, of almost total receptivity where we may become open to the new.